OSLO INTRIGUE

OSLO INTRIGUE

*A Woman's Memoir
of the Norwegian Resistance*

HELEN ASTRUP and B. L. JACOT

McGRAW-HILL BOOK COMPANY, INC.
New York   Toronto   London

This book was first published in Great Britain in 1953 under the title *Night Has a Thousand Eyes.*

Library of Congress Catalog Card Number: 54-9706

Copyright acknowledgments
Plates No. 1 through No. 6, inclusive, courtesy of the authors. Plates No. 7 through No. 12, inclusive, courtesy of the Imperial War Museum, London.

Published by the McGraw-Hill Book Company, Inc.
Printed in the United States of America

To Nils

CONTENTS

ILLUSTRATIONS

FOREWORD

On a september afternoon some years after the war I was walking with my dogs along the stone-flagged passage that winds from Knightsbridge into the comparative solitudes of Rotten Row, when one of the dachshunds discovered something of pressing concern to it in the unsuspecting ankles of a lady a few paces in front. A dachshund is not a dog to be lightly diverted from its avowed intent, and this animal, in addition, was a female; so it fell that my elegant and anonymous fellow stroller became aware of a wet nose applied with Teutonic insistence to her nylons.

She turned with a start, as well she might, and I noted in the split second that here was someone undoubtedly more accustomed to deference than sniffs. The lady obviously spent a good deal of time and no little money on her clothes. She was petite and *soignée* and you could not help noticing her eyes. I fumbled feebly with my hat as I straightened up with the dog under my arm. Then a curious thing happened. We stood looking at each other. A disconcerting, timeless moment seemed to envelop us. At one end of the alley was the rumble and press of London traffic, at the other lay the trees and the grass and a quietude that goes with open skies. Here in the middle, in this alley beside the cavalry barracks of the Household Brigade, was our little enclave. It was as when a film sud-

denly stops, catching and holding the scene frozen, stripped
of the semblance of life and reality.

My thoughts were playing strange tricks with my emo-
tions. I came back to the eyes. They were gray and softly
formed as peat smoke, yet reserved and steady. "It's
Helen," I said.

"The Colonel," she smiled. "Leo!"

The spell dissolved as spells must at the prosaic touch
of the conventions. "Well, I'm sorry about the dog," I
said. The little red bitch was licking my left ear with an
attention to detail that was embarrassing. "What are you
doing in London?"

"I live here," Helen Astrup told me. "You remember
Kirsti? We live together in Sloane Street. Our home."

"But—I live just round the corner in Pont Street," I
said. It seemed incredible that we had not met before.

"Why not put the dog down?" Helen asked.

I replaced my hat and applied two hands to the task of
lowering the dachshund. Years ago—how many?—I had
last seen Helen Astrup in a cellar that reeked of fish cur-
ing. The dawn was not far off and it was bitterly cold. We
were dirty and disheveled—and hungry, too, after a sleep-
less thirty-six hours. In the harbor outside, the German
patrols were shelling, and we thought—wrongly as it happened—that we formed one of the targets, for shells kept
falling uncomfortably close to the fish factory in which
we were trapped. From time to time I would grope my
way to street level to watch the German ships with their
searchlights looking for the visiting Britisher to whom we
had so recently confided certain parcels and wished God-
speed.

"Now is the time to say it's a small world," Helen said.
"It's smaller than that."

There were German troops and *statspoliti* all over the
wharf looking for us and at that time it seemed likely
that they could hardly fail to find us. I had a return ticket
to Scotland endorsed by the Royal Navy, if we got away
from the building uncaught; but Helen, a young widow
who had recently lost her husband, was alone. She had
only her own devices to fall back on. She could have had
worse support, but the situation for her was far from comforting, to say the least of it.

We spent a long night among the fish barrels and
talked of many things. My companion was a good person
to be in a tight corner with; there was little that could
shake her courage. She was young and very attractive,
with wisps of soft blond hair blowing about her rather
grimy face, but I had to acknowledge that she had a little
something extra that I had not. A woman's courage is
quite different from that of a man. It is difficult to say just
how it differs. Perhaps it is more detached and constant.
It seems to hold its flame burning bright without the help
of galvanizing contact with that which is to be fought. A
man's virility blazes up and sinks, like a tomcat's pelt in
a rooftop fight, according to the proximity of the other
cat. A woman's courage is in there fighting all the time.
Woman is more dangerous than man.

"I often wondered what happened to you in the end,"
I said.

"You never came back," she reminded me. Her eyes
are heavily lashed and very level. I could feel them now
traveling over me, looking for marks, maybe.

"It's nine years," I said.

Framed by the elms at the end of the alley was a sun-lit pastiche of ducks on the glinting water of the Serpentine Lake; of children skipping with their hoops on the green spread of the grass; of nurses knitting beside their carriages; of ridden horses stepping high over the loam. "Walk with me for a while," I said. "Tell me what's been happening to you since I saw you last. . . ." And with the three little dogs I was walking beside Helen Astrup again, this time in the heart of London.

Mrs. Astrup was a humble member of a Resistance group in Oslo. She had no outstanding or heroic role to play, but the work this particular group carried out was important. It was of great help to the British and to the Norwegian Army headquarters in London. My work in Norway was liaison in those early and difficult days when the Resistance was scattered and disorganized by betrayals. Helen's job, when I first saw her, was that of getting rid of copies of a Resistance newspaper. I was under the impression for a long time that she was a Norwegian girl. I noted professionally that she was much too attractive (and therefore, conspicuous) to use in the open. I do not remember more of our first meeting. Helen says she wanted to speak to me in English and tell me she was English, but that she was afraid to say anything to me; I looked so forbidding. I do not think we exchanged a word that first time we met at the back of the little tobacco shop in Oslo which is mentioned in this book.

It was through the man Helen calls Nils Berg that I came to work with her eventually. In the end I was relying on her more than I relied on most. The debacle in the fish factory was the end of a job for me. I left Norway. After we parted in the yard of the factory I did not see Helen again, but several of the photographs in the book reached us in London from Helen's group. I presumed she was still with them.

We sat, that afternoon, under the plane rees by the Epstein Memorial to Hudson, the naturalist. Not far away the Labradors trained by the Metropolitan Police were barking in their pens and there were youths rowing and laughing on the lake. It takes time to gather the threads and translate the humdrum present into the idiom of more momentous days. From time to time I made her smile and the flash of her white teeth showed. Helen's skin has a coin-smooth, petallike texture. Her blond hair accentuates a deceptive softness in the line of her neck. There are those who would see in Helen Astrup only the surface that mirrors a delicate profile—and who can blame them? She is one of the most beautiful women I have ever seen. Others more perceptive might guess at the core of spring steel that holds her together. Steel undoubtedly is the basis of her character, but with Helen you would not suspect this—at first.

I was recalling the things we confided long ago among the barrels at that Norwegian fish factory. We were English, the two of us; and we were a long way from home that night. I was conscious of what an attractive young person I was working with. Here in Hyde Park, nine years later, I had to acknowledge she now had something more which I find impossible to describe. Helen had a quality— a maturity that was something I had never been in contact with before.

"You married again?"

She shook her head. I knew what she was thinking as she stared away at the smudge fires the gardeners were tending.

"Your friends in Norway?"

"I go back sometimes," she said. "But it's different. It's not the same now. What happened was so strange it is like a fence. It shuts out the old life. I wouldn't live there again. Sometimes I think of the old times a good deal. And you?"

"A lot has happened since then."

"I'm quite happy as I am," Helen said. "You should see Kirsti! She's taller than me now. And very attractive. But, of course, you must come and meet her again! You're coming back to tea with us."

I went back to the apartment on Sloane Street. It is on the top floor of a new block with a wide view over the London chimney pots away to the Surrey hills. Everything is spick and span, as you would expect with anyone as house-proud as Helen. The furnishings and draperies are luxurious—extravagant even, but Helen herself is still ready at the drop of your hat to roll up her sleeves and busy herself in the kitchen. I met a Kirsti I should never have recognized except for the almost laughable likeness to her mother. I met, too, the famous canary that Helen went back to Norway to fetch—the bird that lived through the Occupation with them. It is mentioned in the book.

In the days that followed I saw a good deal of Helen and Kirsti. Mrs. Astrup was under doctors' treatment for insomnia, which had begun to undermine her health. She slept very badly and was at the point where she dreaded what sleep she was able to get on account of the persistent nightmare that haunted her. It was some time before she told me about it, and certainly it was curious enough to make one hesitate to confide. When she slept the same theme ran through her dreams. These were most vivid, and in them she lived her ordinary, everyday life, but with this difference. If she opened a drawer there would be a dead hand in it. If she felt in her purse, her fingers would touch the cold flesh. If anyone raised his hat to her in her dreams that dead, cold hand would be standing upright on the man's head. At times she would dream of being in a restaurant and the waiter would whip off the cover of a dish with which to serve her . . . and the dish would be this cold, dead hand.

The specialists in Harley whom she consulted told her that all this was the result of what she had been through in the war. She was in a state of anxiety neurosis, they told her. I should have imagined that it was scarcely necessary to go to Harley Street to guess that. The doctors said that time would effect its healing cure and they gave her a prescription for sleeping pills. In spite of this, at the time we met again the dead hand continued to haunt her as faithfully as ever. She was even worse, for a while.

Then we noticed a curious thing. I was seeing her every day now, and after we had spent a late evening over the fire talking about the things that had happened to her so wildly and so incredibly, she tended to sleep like a log, without even a dream, let alone a nightmare. The more she raked up out of the past, the less the hand came to trouble her. There is no doubt about the fact that her health began to improve. Helen came down to stay with us in our country house, in the heart of the Mendips. From one week to the next we never saw an outside soul. Helen and I and the dogs went for long walks among the worked-out lead mines of Roman days—the mine that supplies Bath with some of its plumbing being still in service. We went on picnics to the sands beside the Bristol Channel and bathed at Brean where it is warmer than in the glacier-fed fjords of Norway. Inevitably Helen was thinking of Cherry Trees, the farmhouse that comes so prominently into her story. I am no psychiatrist, but I know that whatever it was that was troubling her inner mind got its *congé* through our talks about the old days. She got something she had been trying for years to re-press right out of her system. She got it all out into the open, and incidentally it gave us the book. You might say that a dead hand chased it up out of the past.

One morning in the spring, I said to her, "You have to write a book."

She shook her head. "It is easy for you to say. Writing is your job. But how would you react if you were suddenly asked—say, to perform a brain operation?"

"Anyone can write a book," I said. "You couldn't help writing a book about what happened to you in Norway."

"Not me."

"I've seen you do most things."

"I couldn't write a book to save my life."

"You are the book yourself," I told her. "The book will be you. I shall make it as much *you* as possible. The rest is just what happened."

She stopped and looked at me keenly. "You said *you*

will make it as much like me as possible. You mean *you* would write the book, if there was going to be one?"

"Why not? At the start of the war I had to interview hundreds of people who had had things happen to them. There would be survivors out of submarines or of aircraft that had been shot down. They used to tell me their stories and I wrote them up for the newspapers."

"The war was different. Everything was different then."

"It was the same war you were in. And things are never different if you have a good story to tell. Just let the people have the facts. They'll listen."

"It doesn't seem real any more. People would never believe what happened in Norway."

"They'll believe it all right. There was a Battle of Britain pilot whose parachute burned out and left him to drop the last three thousand feet free. I interviewed him, too."

"He *survived?*"

"He hit some trees and lived to tell the tale—and nobody I ever heard of disbelieved him."

"You're being clever and trying to trap me into writing this book."

"Helen," I said, "listen! I'll tell you a trade secret about writing books and things. You cannot counterfeit the ring of a story that comes from someone who's telling you of what he's just been through. There's something that comes out and grips you. It's real and all anyone like me has to do is get it down."

"It is nine years ago," Helen said.

"Great painters," I said, "paint from models. You can achieve the same fidelity if you paint out of your own head. If you are in contact with *life,* you get something to pass on you can never get in any other way. The reader senses it by some instinct. All we have to do is to say what happened to you, and to say it in the way you say it to me. Autobiography is real and urgent and *living* because it's at first hand."

"I still say I can't write a book."

"Haven't I just proved that you can? All you have to do is answer my questions. They will guide the book into the form the public expects of such a book."

"What book?"

"The book we are going to write," I told her.

"I am not going to write a book," she said, and that was that.

But some days later she remarked to me, "You were talking about the 'form' of the book. Would that mean the *way* you would write it?"

I told her that it would. "What you have to do," I said, "is tell *me,* keeping your mind on *me.* Never think of the book itself or the readers, or anyone. Tell *me.* I'll set it all down just as you tell it and it will have a quality all its own."

"But I can't even spell!"

"You don't have to write a single word. You can talk, can't you? Half the writers in Hollywood never write a word, couldn't write a word. They're talking writers."

"And the result is moving pictures!"

"Never mind. The principle is the thing. Your personality is going to come out of the book and hit anyone in the face. They'll share your thoughts and feel what you feel. The book will be in your everyday words. If you try to dress the story up in its Sunday best you'll kill it with formality. It will lose its integrity. Nothing in the book is going to 'commence.' What starts, starts. And that is that."

"I don't begin to know what you're talking about."

"For heaven's sake!" I cried. "You've given me most of the book already."

"You mean that what I've been telling you is—the book?"

"What else?"

"But it would have to be something that people would want to read."

"It may even be that. Let's make a start and see how it goes. For instance—where were you and what were you doing when it all began to happen?"

"Where was I?" she echoed, "why, I was. . . ."

It took eight months to sort all the material out. I have tried to write the book faithfully as Helen Astrup told it to me. Some of the material we were not allowed to use. Some of the names we had to change for obvious reasons. There were photographs we were asked to suppress and places we disguised. But the words and the thoughts are Helen's own.

The shortcomings on the writing side are conspicuous, but in fairness there is this to be said. All women tend to repeat themselves. In narrative, they lean toward the passive rather than toward the active and direct. If the story appears to do the same, that is as it should be. Is not a woman telling it?

I set my sights on getting the story into print with the echo of Helen's words still ringing about it. Within the scope of my talent I painted from the model. I can only hope that with such material I could hardly fail at times to come close to the original. It is a task I have been proud to perform.

B. L. JACOT

Radstock,
March, 1954

OSLO INTRIGUE

1

A KNOCK

THAT AFTERNOON in Oslo when the knock came, I was standing at my window, watching the finely powdered snow blow about over the frozen ground in little feathery puffs. War had restricted the activities of most people, and I had a tendency in those days to spend more and more time at the window. My apartment faced an open space that stretched away toward Holmenkollbakken, the place where the famous ski competitions are held each year. That afternoon in February, 1941, when the knock came at the door I was thinking about many things.

At the back of my mind was always the loss of my husband. I still, at times, had the feeling that it could not be true. Then there was the perpetual anxiety about Kirsti, my daughter. I was haunted by the question of what would become of a little girl like her if anything happened to me. I had no doubt she would be put in an institution for turning out young Nazis, with only her Nazi bosses to look to for guidance in the difficult business of life. But the main thing on my mind was a long telephone talk I had just had

3

with someone for whom I had the greatest respect. This was the first time I had known Jan Goffinger to be anxious. There was no reason for him to have telephoned me, except to find out if I was still in circulation. I sensed from the start that he must have heard some rumor that made him nervous. It seemed to me that it must be about our block of apartments, for he kept cross-questioning me like a child about my associations with my neighbors.

Although I was a Norwegian woman through my marriage to a Norwegian, I still had my British nationality and my passport. I was at large in a German-controlled country and the slightest transgression—in theory—could land me in a prison camp employing slave labor. In practice, no one took the slightest notice of me. "Your position is precarious," Jan kept saying. "You must be careful with whom you are seen." I imagined that there had been some outbreak of Resistance activity in our neighborhood and that a search might be made. There had been an incident lately quite close to home in our block. The police had been around making inquiries about a neighbor who was a Jew, but no one spoke about it. No one wished to become involved. The Resistance movement was well organized at that time in Norway; yet no one seemed to know much about what was going on. If the Hirschfeldts were in trouble with the Nazis, most people thought: let them get out of it; we have troubles enough of our own. "You must be particularly careful to do nothing rash," Jan had said.

"I haven't done a thing all afternoon except look out of the window."

"Anything can happen to a woman in this town."

"Anything can happen to her anywhere," I said.

This was scarcely cheerful talk for one who was feeling a little blue already. "Tell me what's bothering you, Jan," I asked. "Why all the fuss today?"

"Will you promise me one thing?" was all he answered. "Especially today, avoid any risks that might lead you into danger."

"What danger?"

"I can't tell you over the telephone," he said, "but— you promise?"

"Of course, Jan. If it makes you any easier in your mind."

"I will be seeing you," Jan told me then. "God bless you!" He rang off.

We had been talking in German, for Jan Goffinger's English was not good—no compliment to me, who had been his tutor in the language for months—and his Norwegian was grotesque. The whole business was very unlike Jan, and it upset me a little to wonder what he had in mind. I was very fond of the tall, immaculate Hollander, always so correct, so grave and formal. He had such authority of manner. He had come to me in the first weeks after I knew my husband was dead and showed kindness and consideration to me when I was in a daze of sorrow. He made life possible for me. He took charge and I simply did what he said. I had need of a man's help.

When my husband Carsten Astrup went down with his ship, he was one of the first Norwegian sea captains in the Allied service to lose their lives. The British gave him command of an oil tanker and it was torpedoed when in convoy off the northeast coast of Ireland. No one informed me for nearly three weeks and to this day the British Admiralty has never notified me. At the time Carsten died, the Germans had not yet attacked Norway, and I had enough income from London to carry on at the apartment. I could not have brought myself to sell out and move somewhere smaller. It was a large place, too big for my little girl and myself, living of course without servants of any kind. But I clung to every little bit of that apartment. I had been so happy there I did not want to see any of it go. Sister Hjoerdis, who worked at the big hospital nearby, said I was foolish to keep even Carsten's old pipes. They would remind me of him all the time, she said. That was just what I wanted. I wanted to cling to that happiness, for I felt in those days that I would have precious little more coming my way. Having Kirsti was a comfort, but it was not the same. If you are truly in love with a man, there is nothing else in life to compare. That can be enough in itself—especially if it is a man like Carsten, a tower of strength with a courage that will break anything that comes against it. You are born only once. You can only die once. I believe that when you give your heart to a man it is like that. Carsten meant everything to me, and more than half my life went with him when he sank with his ship.

The apartment was expensive. When the Nazis came marching into Oslo in April, 1940, my London income ceased. Carsten's people were put in concentration camps or, like his uncle, a very rich man, voluntarily disappeared, and I was therefore a young widow on her own, unemployable on account of her nationality, yet with a child to keep alive on a ration diet of occasional pieces of coarse bread, and issues of turnips and the like. There was no milk, no meat or fish, no tea, coffee, or any form of drink except water; with occasional electricity for light, practically none for heat, and only such wood to burn as you yourself could find and carry. Few people realize that Norway came very close to mass starvation during the German occupation. There simply was not sufficient for the people to eat, and it cost a fortune in money and miles and miles of weary walking to feed a child on the black market. Thanks to the help of Jan Goffinger, with his connections in the diplomatic corps, I managed to feed Kirsti and keep the apartment.

Carsten and I had first met in Bath, which I still think is the loveliest town in England and the world. Carsten was twenty-nine when he was lost at sea in a burning tanker. He died like many of his ancestors, for as long as records went back his people had been seamen and shipowners. He was a remarkable-looking man. He stood four inches over six feet and was as blond as an ashplant. He had a huge laugh and my most poignant memory of him is the way he met every situation with it, hilarious or otherwise. Once when we were out driving together up in the mountains in the new American car we had just bought, he misjudged a curve and hit the rails. Carsten was thrown into the top of a pine tree and the first thing that came to my ears after the sound of the crash had subsided was my husband's echoing mirth. You could hear his roar of laughter clean across the valley. An elderly doctor who once set Carsten's ankle when he broke it skiing confided, "I can't understand this chap. He seems to think it funny." Nothing ever upset Carsten. His skin was always very tanned and against it his eyes showed blue and seaman-clear. It made his teeth look very

white. At the corners of his eyes were a thousand fine
wrinkles drawn there by his laughter.

I had not long left school when I met Carsten. He was
staying with the family of a business connection of his uncle
in Bristol. We did all the things young folk in love will do—
we danced, we had picnics, we walked in the hills and swam
in the sea, but mostly we went out sailing together. Although it was two years before we were married in Oslo,
there never was any other man for me from the moment I
first saw Carsten. His people had a line of ships plying between Bergen and Bristol and roughly every month Carsten
would arrive in Bristol and call me up. He was an appren-
tice mate on his uncle's ship and I used to exist in between
telephone calls. In those early days I scarcely knew what I
was doing for thinking of Carsten. My mother said I used
to walk into things and did not answer when spoken to. I
think we both understood from the first that some day we
would be married, for it is a fact that Carsten never pro-
posed to me. We just got married as soon as he received his
first command, and I almost died of sheer happiness on the
long journey out to my wedding in one of the company's
ships captained by a rival skipper. My wedding day was
the happiest day of my life. It always will be, for nothing
can take away the memory.

We had nearly six years together, too happy to last, in
our home overlooking Holmenkollbakken and at Larkollen, the farmhouse that once belonged to Carsten's grandmother, where we used to spend summer months whenever
we could manage between Carsten's trips. Now all was
changed, but I still got out occasionally to our country
place, for in the warmer months, when the roads were us-

able and the farms were not frozen up solid, it was possible to get food from the farmers. I used to walk miles round the district exchanging warm clothing for bacon and ham. People in the hills did not want money but they badly needed clothing; even at that early time in the war there were many in Norway who halked about in wooden-soled shoes, even paper-soled footwear, and that is no joke in a country with a climate like Norway's.

Someone knocked.

2

TWEEDLEDUM AND
TWEEDLEDEE

I WALKED to the door wondering who it might be, for it was too early to expect Kirsti home from school. Suddenly I did not want to open it; in fact, I had the notion to run and hide, but the impossibility of doing any such thing impressed itself on me and I told myself my nerves were beginning to make a fool out of me. "You're getting scared of every shadow," I said to myself. "You look twice at any man in the road and anyone who looks up at your windows in passing gives you three fits. Soon every single noise will be the Germans coming to take you away from Kirsti." I pulled myself together and opened the door.

Two German officers were there on the doormat. My hand flew to my mouth. I think they had been listening to my footfall on the other side of the door and wished to scare me into the right frame of mind. They certainly succeeded! I was virtually paralyzed. I had worked myself up to it so successfully with my afternoon's brooding.

"You are Fru Astrup," the smaller of the two Germans

said. His eyes were on me like those of some fish. The Germans never asked questions. They made statements and dared you to contradict them.

"Yes," I said in Norwegian. I wasn't going to speak English or even German, for I speak it with an English schoolgirl accent. "Is—is something wrong?"

This pair was very smartly dressed, as were most of the German officers at that time of the occupation. Their gloves looked brand new and the set of their high-crowned hats was elegant. The belts outside their greatcoats were polished like glass. But I hated every shred of them. The taller one began to talk now, and while he spoke the other one half-withdrew from his pocket what I clearly saw to be a photograph. He sneaked a look at it and lifted his eyes quickly to my face. I knew then that he had met the woman he was looking for.

"May we enter your house, gracious lady?" the German asked with a stiff bow. He had that cold, Prussian, sadistic face, and the politeness of his form of address confirmed my worst fears. I am not a bold and resourceful person who can improvise. Personal danger leaves me helpless. I do not seem to be able to think. I could only stand back and let them enter now. The Germans walked stiffly in, saluting as they came. "This is it," I told myself. "It's happened."

As the two men moved across the threshold I could see down the hall. By the elevator, gathered into a knot, was a sinister group of civilians. They had the look of civil servants or plain-clothes men and they were of the same party, evidently waiting. Quisling police, I thought. A little man in a raincoat saw me watching, and he began to approach;

so I left the door hurriedly and followed the Germans into my sitting room with my heart in my mouth.

The two officers were standing by the open fireplace with their Nazi hats still under their arms, like Tweedledum and Tweedledee. Their eyes were wandering round the room, and I recognized the look of appreciation. "You have a charming apartment, Fru Astrup," the older man said. "The water colors are of England, are they not?"

"I am English and I painted them myself." I thought a little culture would do no harm.

"So? Charming! Charming! Isn't this the Royal Crescent at Bath?"

"It is." To one born and brought up in Bath, Royal Crescent was more or less a natural. I did not like the way the smaller man was watching me. It made me feel that all this was a trap. For the life of me I could not imagine what the trap might be. But I was not going to deny Bath for anyone.

"Your books are English, too."

"I have lived in Oslo for some years. Seven to be precise. A German U-boat sank my husband's ship and I am a widow."

My questioner made a slight inclination. I found out later from Jan that he was a full colonel, formerly in the regular cavalry, and as far as I was concerned he was polite, even sympathetic—on the surface at any rate.

"You have always lived here, Madame?"

"We have a summer retreat on the fjord at Larkollen, near Moss—about sixty kilometers away by water, but it is only a farmhouse and in winter is cut off. It would be impossible with a small daughter to—to live there permanently."

"But you have a very comfortable home here, Fru Astrup. A modern apartment, high up, in a new building. It is a large apartment for two people."

"Here it comes!" I told myself. It seemed probable from the genteel and polite way the conversation was being carried on that this colonel was about to suggest he should be my guest, with perhaps his batman sleeping in the nurse's room next to my kitchen.

"You are very fair for a Jewess," the major suddenly said. I was to know this familiar police method of abrupt confronting fairly well later, but it startled me at the time.

"I am a Christian," I said.

The colonel made a motion to the other. It seemed that even then he was a little worried about things. This was not quite what he expected. "So your friend Herr Goffinger said. Your Dutch friend—you remember?"

Jan! I hoped that he had not got himself into any trouble with the Germans. Although very polished, he could be arrogant and intolerant and he did not like being ordered about.

"I give Mr. Goffinger lessons in English."

"That we know."

I wondered then if they knew he paid me in precious gold. Some time previously he had confided in me that he had a store of gold coins—"just in case," he said—and he paid for his lessons by letting me have an English sovereign or a French gold piece from time to time, advising me to put it away and keep it ready to use in emergency. "Gold goes anywhere, any time."

"We are not concerned with Mr. Goffinger," the colonel told me, and I breathed again. I think merely having gold was an offense, and at that moment my offense could have been turned up without much difficulty in the bathroom. "I have reason to believe that you may be able to help us in a little matter the local people here would not understand."

I said nothing. I was thinking that Kirsti would soon be coming home from school, and she had the habit of blurting out the first thing that came into her head. Most of the Norwegian children among themselves alluded to the Germans as *svina*. Kirsti was quite capable of calling them that to their faces. She often caused me embarrassment in streetcars and trains by the things she said. Norwegian, of course, was her native tongue, but she also spoke English as her second language, and I never quite knew what she would say, in which language, and when. I certainly did not want Kirsti walking in on this now.

"I don't know what I could do to help you," I said.

"You could be of great help to us, Fru Astrup. You have the character and you are the type."

The colonel caught the eye of his major and they inclined in little bows, like owls on a twig. The Germans are sometimes so obvious. In this instance, you could almost hear the words, "I have your approval, Herr Tweedledum?" "With my compliments and best respects, Herr Tweedledee—go ahead. Put it to her that way."

"We try to behave correctly and fairly to all concerned in this unfortunate situation," the colonel said. "But the Norwegians have not always understood us, or our intentions. In fact, they show a certain amount of hostility which we did not expect."

I said nothing. I thought for the moment that they must want me to make propaganda broadcasts in English.

"The Norwegians as a whole do not understand about the Jews," he said. "We had a report that you were a Jewess, you see. You have Jewish friends—no?"

I had many friends in Oslo and some of them were Jews, but I thought I knew then whom he was talking about. I waited for his next words with some anxiety.

"Your neighbors in this block of apartments, Fru Astrup. The Hirschfeldts. I take it that you know the Jew Hirschfeldt has disappeared?"

I shook my head. This was news to me—distressing news.

"He was ordered to report at the railway station for work in Germany and he has chosen to abandon his family and disappear. I think you will be able to help us find him, and that will be better for all, particularly for the family he has left behind."

Hirschfeldt was a prominent man—a lawyer—and I knew, as everyone did in our block, that he had been called up by the Germans and questioned on several occasions.

"When did he disappear?" I asked them.

"Sometime in the night. He was to report himself at six o'clock this morning. Our men have searched their apartment, of course—and now . . . with your kind permission? We may search here?"

It was no secret that I liked Fru Hirschfeldt very much and that I had cause to be grateful to her, but I could see no reason why they should suppose her husband was in my bathroom or somewhere. I had nothing to conceal, however, and I was not afraid of anything they might find.

"You may search my apartment if you wish," I said, "but the idea that Herr Hirschfeldt is here is ridiculous."

They bowed and left me and I heard the major speaking to someone in a low tone at the front door—evidently calling in assistance from his thugs. Some of the Jews in Oslo had been beaten up by the Germans, and I myself had seen one who had been "under treatment" as they called it. He was a pleasant little *vaktmester*—concierge or janitor— from a nearby block of apartments. When they released him he had lost an eye, and his foot was so badly crushed it had to be amputated later in our hospital at Ullevaal.

I was beginning to get frightened. Fru Hirschfeldt was a tiny little woman who would not have hurt a fly. She had a little girl the age of Kirsti and in the same class at school. They always went to school together and came back in the same group. The Hirschfeldts were kind, gentle, and tolerant; and the thought of Herr Hirschfeldt in the hands of the Nazis made me shudder. In addition I was quite sure that between the two of them they had saved my life when I was ill only a few weeks previously. Fru Hirschfeldt never left my side for three days, and the food they could produce made all the difference—that and Sister Hjoerdis's nursing. During the crisis they took Kirsti off my hands, and I believe it was as much that weight off my mind as anything that got me through.

I was praying now, as I heard the search going on, that Herr Hirschfeldt had been smart enough to get away. Once he had done that, the Resistance people would look after him. Their rapid organization was one of the surprises the invading Germans had in store for them. In our district of the town the Joessings* were strong—almost anyone could tell you what to do to get in touch with someone who wished the Germans no good. At this time I had no active contact with the underground movement, although, like all good Norwegians, I obstructed the Quislings privately to the extent of my opportunities—when I knew who they were.

The man in the raincoat came up while I was waiting and suddenly said to me, "I suppose you know that you should not be living in this large apartment all by yourself." He was an educated Norwegian.

"I have my daughter," I said.

"Mother and child are together allowed one room. One room for each other adult child. You have read the proclamation issued by the government?"

I thought then that if I started an argument with this man I would land up being questioned at Victoria Terrasse, the Gestapo headquarters, and I did not want to be taken away while this rummaging in my cupboards was going on.

"I have read it, of course," I said. "And in these times I agree that such things are necessary. But I have some nurses from the Ullevaal Hospital who live here with me." I thought quickly. "Four. They happen to be on duty now at the hospital."

The colonel came back with his major and they both looked rather uncomfortable. "We thank you, gracious

* From the very first days those patriots who banded themselves together to work against the Nazis were called Joessings, after the brave man who sank a German ship in Norwegian home waters.

lady," the colonel said. "I trust you will forgive us for the nuisance we have been."

"You found Herr Hirschfeldt?" I asked.

"He is not here," he answered seriously. "We wish you good-by, Fru Astrup."

I stood in my sitting room by my little grand piano and listened to them tramping out of my home. I did not know it then, but I was already drawn into the mesh. After I had heard the elevator go down on the landing outside I went to my front door and shut it. Then I sat down on the sofa and had a good, satisfying cry. I was weeping like a fool when Kirsti let herself into the apartment with her own personal key of which she was so proud.

3

THE MOVING DOORMAT

AFTER THE Germans had left me that afternoon I knew I had to get into contact with Fru Hirschfeldt. She would need any help that could be given her. When my daughter got home I gave her her evening meal in the kitchen and then explained what had happened to Herr Hirschfeldt. I told her we had to pay a visit to Fru Hirschfeldt and take her some food. I doubted whether she would leave the apartment to go shopping, and it was quite likely that she and her little girl Sara might already be in difficulties. I told Kirsti the Germans had called to see me, but I did not dwell on it for I did not want to scare her. She was bound to hear from the neighbors that the Germans had been around, so I hastened to tell her so myself. "It was a very nice colonel," I said.

Kirsti looked at me and said nothing. Evidently she had her own opinion about this.

"I have to go around to the hospital first and try to find Sister Hjoerdis. She will be coming to live with us. Remember to say she is living with us if anyone asks you.

"I told the Germans we had four nurses living with us. They would have taken our apartment away from us, perhaps, if they thought we were living here by ourselves. So we have to get four nurses, and you shall come with me if you are good. Afterward we will pack some food for Fru Hirschfeldt and Sara."

"Sara was not at school today."

"She is staying at home for a while with her mother," I said.

I went with Kirsti that evening to the Ullevaal Hospital and asked for Sister Hjoerdis, an old friend of Carsten's and mine who often spent her vacations on the fjord at Larkollen. She was dark-eyed and with her beautiful black hair she looked anything but Norwegian. How cheerful and capable she was! At the moment Hjoerdis was busy with the surgeon and could not come down, but she arranged to meet me in half an hour at the Ullevaal Stadium. So Kirsti and I walked the streets and parks together, as we often did in those days—for exercise and entertainment, since there was precious little else to do in Oslo.

In due course Hjoerdis joined us and I explained the situation to her. To my relief she was only too glad to come and live with us, and she arranged on the spot to bring three girls along with her. I was feeling better by now, but we still had to call on Fru Hirschfeldt. I thought the best and most innocent way was to call openly, so I told Kirsti what we had to do—for a child of eight she had to learn a lot of things about life and learn them quickly, poor mite—and we packed as much food as we could spare into a basket. I warned Kirsti not to speak English—when frightened or excited she had a tendency to speak English without realizing.

We closed our own front door and walked down the stairs. I held on tight to my daughter's hand, imagining half a dozen eyes riveted on my back. Those arrogant and all-powerful men tramping over my beautiful carpets had done something to my confidence. I knew it was not very wise to be helping a Jewish family that was in trouble, but I did not think anyone would make a case out of my well-meant action. The block was silent and the corridors empty. I was very innocent then! I even said in a voice anyone could hear, if listening, "It is only neighborly to see if Fru Hirschfeldt needs something for her child to eat."

At the Hirschfeldt's front door I put the basket down. I held my finger out to press the bell. But before my finger could touch it I felt something move under my foot as my weight shifted to the doormat, and a distant buzzing sounded downstairs in the hall.

Then Kirsti and I were flying, as if the devil himself were after us. Clutching the basket in one hand and holding Kirsti with the other, we were back in our apartment, it seemed, in one flying swoop. I have never moved so fast in my life.

After I had shut our front door and shot the bolts I stood with my ear against the panels, listening. I heard steps running up the stairs from below. It seemed there were two men in heavy boots. They stopped on the floor below, and after a while I heard a door open and shut. After that there were no further sounds. No steps came in our direction, so Kirsti and I made a pot of herb tea in the kitchen.

"I wonder if that was your nice colonel," Kirsti said.

The rest of the night I spent on tenterhooks. Even after I had locked up and gone to bed I could not get to sleep for some time. I lay awake thinking of Herr Hirschfeldt. I wondered where he was and if Fru Hirschfeldt had heard anything from him as to whether he was safe or not. In the end I dozed off.

I woke up suddenly after I do not know how long to a strange but very real conviction that there was someone in the room with me. I lay still, with every muscle tensed, quite unable to move. It was as though I were in the grip of one of those horrible nightmares where any movement is impossible and dreadful things impend. I told myself, "Wake up! You are only dreaming as a result of the nerve-racking time you have just been through. Wake up and relax!"

I compelled myself to move my shoulder and raise my neck—although it cost me a supreme effort and was only achieved by placing implicit faith in reason and logic against all urging of instinct. Logic said there could not be anyone in the room. Instinct said: *He's there!*

I began to look round and a voice said, "If you are awake, Helen, don't be scared. It's only me—Nils."

My heart stopped beating, it seemed, ages before. I could not see anyone. "If anything happens I shall scream!" I said weakly. It was the senseless sort of thing you say when your mind is not working properly through shock, but to hear myself say anything—however silly—was comforting.

A big shape drifted closer to the bed and then I felt in some strange way reassured. Nils said softly, "Don't be alarmed. This is very urgent or I would not have risked frightening you." It was indeed Nils Berg.

"How did you get here?" I whispered. "I locked up everything securely." One of the first things I had done when the Germans came marching in was to have an extra lock fitted on my door, together with two long steel bolts.

"I came up the veranda at the back. The *vaktmester* here is working with us."

"Who's us?"

"Why, Helen," he said. "The Joessings, of course. We've been watching this block. Since the Germans came to search the Hirschfeldts' apartment and took Fru Hirschfeldt and the little girl, we've been here keeping an eye on things."

I was thoroughly awake now and my heart sank. To think of Fru Hirschfeldt in the hands of the Germans! I debated with myself whether I would tell Nils how I had tried to help her, but decided to keep my own counsel. "They've taken her away?" I echoed.

"You have a lot of Quislings in this block. You must be more careful. We know you tried to ring their bell tonight. Didn't you realize how dangerous that would be?"

"How would it be dangerous to do a neighborly act like that?"

"Surely you realize that in a case where the husband disappears they would take the wife and child away and lie in wait for any confederates who might turn up? You have had a very lucky escape. One of our people saw you go down but no one else did. The Germans found no one there when they rushed up, and they think it was a false alarm, for we saw them going over the wiring of that contraption of theirs. In fact, we shorted it for them again, just to convince them such things could happen. See?"

I did not see but I let him go on.

"You might easily be at Victoria Terrasse by now. You must never do anything like that again."

"I only wanted to help Fru Hirschfeldt," I said.

"You can help her," Nils said. "But don't try to do it on your own. You don't know what you're up against. And, anyway, that's what we're here for. Now—just go to sleep again. I shall go the way I came and no one will see a thing. Don't worry! We've got an eye on you and we won't let anything happen. I suppose you'd like to be some help?"

"Of course I would."

"With us Joessings?"

"With you more than anyone."

Nils came closer. "Well, living here in this block you could at that. Listen—think it over and if you still want to help, all you have to do is to come to the tobacconist's in Bogstadveien and ask anyone who's behind the counter if they have any American cigarettes. Don't say it if there're a lot of people in the shop. But there never are, always just one person behind the counter, and remember—American cigarettes."

"I'll remember," I promised.

Nils Berg had been a close friend of my husband's. They were schoolmates. He was a gray-eyed, heavy, lumbering man, a real son of Oslo, who worked as a serviceman for a company, originally American, which supplied Oslo with most of its home refrigerators. The job was still going on, for someone had to attend to the refrigerators even though no new ones were coming in. He often came around to see me at the apartment. He had access to a mysterious store of hard liquor and he seldom arrived without a bottle of aquavit or schnapps. He also never came without a cargo of the latest gossip. It had always surprised me, until I got to know him better, what an old woman for gossip he was.

He was a bachelor without any known relatives, and his opinion of my sex was not high. He never spoke of it or even admitted it by implication, but Carsten once told me that when he was very young he was desperately in love with a girl who suddenly decided to ditch him for a much richer man, and from that day Nils never looked at another woman.

There was a good deal of solid comfort in Nils. He treated me as a child to a certain extent, whereas Jan treated me invariably as something fragile and exotic, whose perfumed hand was to be kissed reverently. On the whole, I preferred Nils's approach, although at times the other attitude can bring great comfort. Nils had no culture to speak of. I do not think he had ever read any book for pleasure. Yet he was possessed of sound common sense of the sort that makes living much easier. I would have made no important move without asking Nils what he thought about it. It might take him days to decide, but when you got the answer it would probably be the right one. In addition to all his sterling qualities and his doglike fidelity—I think he had some chivalrous idea he had to look after his dead friend's rather frivolous and empty-headed widow— Nils had the most useful attribute of being able to fix almost anything at all. He could repair the most unlikely objects and he could make anything work. What is more, he could generally manage it with odd tools and bits and pieces to be found in his pockets.

Yes, there was a great deal of comfort in Nils, and particularly right at this time, although it had been a shock when he showed up from nowhere in the middle of the night like that. He may have been clumsy-looking, but this time he was as sly as a fox, and in the same way he was gone before I knew it. I lay there thinking about what he had said, until I decided at last to go around the next day and ask for the American cigarettes.

4

"NILS SENT ME"

AFTER I HAD sent Kirsti off to school next morning I wrapped myself up warmly in an old coat and walked round to the little shop on Bogstadveien. I passed it twice before I plucked up courage and entered. It was a small shop with a door communicating with a living room at the back. The counter was laden with the usual sort of glass showcases; behind it was a young girl. No one else was in the shop. I had made sure of this before entering, and now I heard myself asking in an absurdly forced and theatrical voice, "Have you any American cigarettes?"

The girl reached up and handed me a packet without comment; then, as I still stood there, she asked, "Anything else?"

I said—quite wrongly from the point of view of security and indeed against the strict rules, "Nils sent me."

This girl was Margit Christiansen, whose aunt owned the shop, one of the most level-headed and the coolest of persons. She beckoned me into the room at the back and there I found two young men who eyed me in silence. The

27

older of the two then questioned me for a while and I explained about Fru Hirschfeldt and how I wished to help her after all she had done for me in my own sickness.

"We cannot decide that here," I was told. "Never mention names in the shop. But you may come again later. Come any time and if you find anyone else in the shop buy cigarettes and go. Come to the shop any time you like. You could help us in that block where you live."

"I am quite ready to do so."

"There are plenty of the other sort living there—*svina.*"

I thought then that to help these people would give me something to do. Life would be more exciting, and naturally, too, I wanted to do anything I could that would hurt the Germans.

Before I left I had a talk with Margit and undertook to distribute the Resistance newssheet. This was a mimeographed typewritten sheet—seldom turned out in the same place for more than a few days at a time before it was then moved on to some other attic or shed or cellar—giving the real news, mostly as put out by the BBC. Hundreds of copies were run off and distributed, among other things giving people instructions how to sabotage the Germans and the Quislings to best effect. Turning out this newssheet was a dangerous job and the Nazis were anxious to catch those responsible.

Copies of the newssheet were scarce and people passed them on to those they could trust. If caught by the Quislings or the Nazis in possession of the newssheet, you were sent automatically to a prison camp. The Norwegian policeman patrolling our district usually brought us a copy and later collected it, but this would generally be a somewhat ancient issue that had already passed through dozens of hands.* Copies fresh from the press or duplicating machine were distributed from Margit's shop. Large rewards were posted for information leading to the arrest of those putting out these sheets.

As I was walking home that morning I suddenly thought of an old bicycle we had in the cellar. When I was newly married I had bought myself an English machine which I had sent from Bath. The Dutch machines they use in Norway for some reason weigh about a ton and are very difficult on hills. I was proud of my lovely, lightweight English bicycle and had been out for several rides round Holmenkollbakken before Carsten returned from his next trip. He did not like the idea of the bicycle at all. He thought it unladylike; there was also the manlike reason that, like most sailors, he was not a conspicuously good performer with such as horses, skis, and bicycles. I knew I had done wrong again.† The bicycle was put in the cellar and I had barely given it a thought since. Now I decided to get it out and, if the tires held, to ride it around with the Resistance newssheets in the basket over the front wheel. I planned to hide the sheets under my shopping.

The bicycle turned out to be in good order, and the caretaker of our block got it out, oiled it, and pumped up the tires. I sailed off to the shop in Gogstadveien and so

* This obliging policeman also provided us with face creams and French perfume and lipsticks—strange things happened in Oslo under the Nazis!

† My first married mistake was to cut my long blond hair short like the Norwegian girls. When Carsten came back from Bristol and saw me, he was too mad to talk!

began my job as a kind of roundsman. Most days I would walk boldly out of the shop, if the coast were clear, dump the load of papers in my basket, then cycle off.

Cycling was a good way of avoiding attention. Pedestrians were occasionally stopped on the sidewalks and motorists at control points on the roads. Cyclists came between and no one troubled much about them. Further, it was easy to spot a control ahead and turn, either back on your tracks or down some path or side street. I had a regular route of shops and houses and I used to go around unmolested, leaving a bundle here and few there.

One day I had left my cycle at the gate of the house of a man who worked at the central telephone exchange. Mueller was a key worker in the Resistance. I never met him but I was told that it was important to get the sheet to him regularly. His wife was a very talkative woman—a peasant from the far north. She liked to give me a cup of mint tea when I called, and I could scarcely refuse although talking with her was rather a strain. She once asked me if before the war we had milk, too, in England. When I told her that the custom of drinking milk had indeed reached those distant shores she said, "Fancy!" The people in some parts of Norway are sterling in character and have hearts of gold but they are close to the soil and no intellectual giants.

When I came out of the house this particular day, to my horror I saw two Nazi soldiers standing by my cycle. One was peering down to read the name of the maker, which was written under a sort of shield just below the handlebars. Several hundred copies of the newssheet, fresh from the duplicators, lay within two inches of his spectacled face.

If I abandoned the machine and walked off, I thought these men would go to the house and ask questions. Fru Mueller was so dumb she might say anything. I had to stick to the bicycle and get it away. All this flashed through my mind as I turned the corner of the short drive and virtually fell over the Germans.

"This is your cycle," the older one said, and I nodded.

"It is an English machine?"

"Yes. We had many in Oslo before the war. They are good machines . . . expensive, but good."

"That is so," the German told me. He was middle-aged and he had a hideously fat face, with pig eyes that meant— I was sure—a beastlike nature.

"The English make good bicycles," the younger German admitted. "Motorcycles especially so. Is it not, Fraulein?"

"The English are pigs," I said happily. This looked as if it was working up into a nice cozy chat. But with the Germans you can never tell where you are. There are good and there are bad.

In any event, this pig-eyed monster who had me in his power turned his look on me now and I saw that there actually were tears in his eyes.

"When I was a little boy," he said in a voice that would have melted anyone's heart, "I always wanted a bicycle like the other boys in my neighborhood. I had no parents. I lived with my Aunt Julie and we were so poor. Aie, aie, aie! She was so poor. Sometimes I would dream of a new English bicycle. The English make good bicycles. I would dream sometimes that I had an English bicycle and that I bought an English bicycle for my Aunt Julie and with our English bicycles we would—"

"Psst!" the younger man interrupted. "We have to get back to the *häus.*"

"I never had a bicycle when I was a boy," the German told me. The tears were running down his cheeks. "I have never had a bicycle. Not ever! I have always wanted a bicycle. A good English bicycle. The English bicycles—"

At this point the younger man dragged him off, but I could still hear him moaning about good English bicycles as they disappeared down the road.

After this, if I had to go into a house or a shop or a factory for any length of time I either took my load of papers in with me, or took the bicycle in too. The curious thing about the incident was not that I was worried because I could have been taken off to a prison camp, but that I had a genuine and honest urge to offer my machine to the German. He was fat, middle-aged, in a war he hated, I expect; and he was a long way from home. I would gladly have given him the bicycle at that moment. The Germans, as I said, are a peculiar race. I am sure that one was very good to his aunt, anyway.

I distributed the Resistance sheet without incident for some time and I gained a priceless advantage from my connection. The Resistance at that date either plundered German stores on a wholesale scale or, more probably, had access to corrupt German quartermasters who sold their stores. Food was so scarce in Norway that the temptation for the Germans must have been great. The Resistance men and women got German rations. After all these hungry months, Kirsti and I had sausage and the delicious canned veal the Wehrmacht issued for the troops, canned vegetables, canned Danish butter and bacon. In return for my not very important service in riding round the town on my cycle I was allowed precious food. If this is the occupation, Kirsti thought, let it go on forever.

She never knew, of course, of my bicycle excursions, although she may have wondered how I got chilblains on my hands and feet. Riding a bicycle in a Norwegian winter is no joke. Only your knees seem to move in cycling, while the rest of you freezes.

Soon a code was set up for me at the shop in Bogstadveien. No one trusted telephones, which were tapped. If I was wanted at the shop, someone would ring up from the dry cleaner's in our block and say something was ready to collect. It must have been about two weeks after Nils's visit to my bedroom that I had a message from the dry cleaner's which said my white chiffon was ready. I went straight round to Bogstadveien. Nils was there to greet me and he was grinning all over. "We have something upstairs that will interest you," he said.

I had seen Nils since his visit but I had not spoken of my trip to the shop or indeed of the work I was doing. Everything was so cagey and cautious, I thought it was best to say nothing; then I couldn't go far wrong. I had had one big surprise from Nils when he told me that Hjoerdis was a Joessing, and had been a valuable member of the group from the first. I could scarcely believe it; never for a moment had I imagined it. She was the chief contact with the Ullevaal Hospital, where a good deal of Resistance work was organized. One of the doctors there was of immense

value to the underground organization, and Hjoerdis was
the link with this outstanding patriot.

Nils took me up the narrow stairs. In a tiny room at the
top was Herr Hirschfeldt, who greeted me warmly.

"Thank you for what you tried to do for Herta and
Sara," he said.

There was a stupid lump in my throat, and I could not
speak. I had been picturing him as tortured—with an eye
knocked out—and my relief at seeing him whole was intense.

"I don't like this scheme at all," he kept saying to Nils.
"Tell them that I don't want to risk anything happening to
them."

It turned out that everything was ready to send Herr
Hirschfeldt over the frontier into Sweden, but he would
not leave his wife behind. The Gestapo had taken Fru
Hirschfeldt and the daughter to a camp for Jewish women
made of temporary huts not far away. The Resistance had
arranged for her to be "ill" and taken to the hospital. At
this time there were not many Jewish women in the camp
and it was comparatively easy, for the medical officer of the
camp was Doctor Halvorsen, the kingpin of the group at
Ullevaal Hospital—the man with whom Hjoerdis was
working. I was called into a council that had just started.
There were eight men and Sister Hjoerdis, besides myself.
My job was outlined. When I heard what was being dis-
cussed I was startled, to say the least.

The Joessings had learned that Hans Hirschfeldt was
to be shot when picked up. Hirschfeldt was a man with a
European reputation as a jurist and the Resistance groups
were determined to save him. To carry out our plan, *Fru*

Hirschfeldt had to die. Her body was to be taken to the mortuary by two of the hospital porters who were Joessings. The man in charge of the mortuary was of Jewish origin, Rudolf Hitchmann, also a Joessing.

I was horrified to hear Hjoerdis speaking so calmly of putting a patient "to sleep."

"Her Jewish relations," she said, "would be too frightened to come to the Ullevaal Hospital and see to the removal of the body for the burial. Don't the Nazis know that Fru Astrup is her friend? She has already gone out of her way to help her in life and Fru Astrup's record is neutral and beyond suspicion. *She is the one to get the coffin.*"

I felt sick to the pit of my stomach. I knew I could not act like a ghoul over the body of my dead neighbor—and what of little Sara, the daughter? I began rather indignantly to say I could see no sense in the plan and I would have nothing to do with it, when it was discovered that no one had explained to me that Fru Hirschfeldt would be a "living" corpse. She and her daughter would leave the hospital inside one of the rough pine coffins supplied to the Germans by a well-known Oslo furnishing firm of cooperating Quislings.

Fru Hirschfeldt was tiny and she and Sara would only have to lie quiet until I had claimed the body and got it onto a truck.

"A dead Jew is of no interest to the Germans," Nils said. "You have only to present yourself to the hospital social worker's office, sign for the body, then go on the truck around to a yard in Grefsen. Our men will look after you there, but you will be alone on the truck with the driver—who knows nothing of what all this is about and is therefore safe. In case you are stopped by the Nazis—and it is almost certain you will be stopped—everything is genuine. Your pass, your papers—everything!"

Everything except that coffin, I was thinking.

"When is this?" I asked.

"Tomorrow night. You will be fetched. Tell no one, of course, not even Kirsti."

"Who will look after Kirsti while—"

"I shall be in the apartment," Hjoerdis said.

"Who will look after her *if*—"

"There isn't going to be any 'if,' " Nils told me.

5

THE COFFIN IN
THE SNOW

It was shortly after ten o'clock the next evening when Hjoerdis came home to the apartment. Protected by her card issued by the Germans, she could come
and go in the curfew. She took me, warmly wrapped up
against the bitter wind and driving, powdered ice, back to
the street door, where a big American truck was waiting.
She motioned for me to get in and squeezed my hand. The
truck began to move, crunching over the snow.

Inside the cab there was a smell of warm oil and the
windshield wipers had swept out twin segments of clear
glass. The roads were empty and very quiet. Every now
and then I would see a German soldier or a German patrol
on a motorcycle and sidecar. I did not dare look at the
driver, who was not one of "us." It seemed a routine business to him, but I felt as if my heart were trying to choke
me. I hoped I would not fail.

We arrived without being questioned and were then
stopped by a Quisling policeman at the hospital gates. He
had two German soldiers with him and the driver showed

them a pass. "Round the back," the policeman said. I got out of the cab and walked up the steps into the social worker's office.

It was the end of a corridor, the floor of which gleamed like glass. I knocked on the door several times without answer, so finally I opened it and crept in. Behind a desk set across the corner of the room was a stern woman in hospital dress. Her hair was blond, with features you so often see in the Nordic type—everything protruding.

I shall never forget her face, for here right at the start of my mission I had a bad twenty minutes. I still do not like the look of persons with prominent eyes. They remind me too nearly of the Quisling lady social worker of Ullevaal Hospital.

The good lady did not look up from a huge book in which she was apparently engrossed. I sat down in a chair facing the desk and waited. I concentrated on trying not to seem too alert and eager. I was supposed to be numbed with shock and sorrow. I watched those prominent lips, the receding chin, the codlike eyes behind the large glasses, then I dropped my own eyes to the linoleum and just waited. Perhaps she was one of us? Perhaps she was just hanging on to see whether all was clear—whether there were going to be any complications about the truck, before committing herself to action?"

Suddenly she looked up and noticed me for the first time. I am sure I startled her just as much as she startled me. "Well?" she said at length. Life shut down in Oslo with the curfew, and it was indeed surprising to have a visit from a civilian who came from "outside" at so late an hour.

"If you please," I answered. "The porter at the door

sent me to you and it says on the door of the office here—"

"You are being discharged from the hospital?"

This woman, I was thinking, *is* a Quisling. She had a hard look—efficient, unemotional, and calculating. A calculating fish and one to beware of. I dabbed at my eyes with my handkerchief. "Fru Hirschfeldt," I said.

"Who?"

"The late Fru Hirschfeldt."

"Well, why didn't you say so at first? She died here to-day? Any post-mortem?"

This was something I had not been briefed for. In any event, I did not know what an answer either way would mean to our plans. I shook my head vacantly. "They told me I should fetch her."

"Who told you? You had a letter?"

"It was a telephone message. I don't know who spoke on the telephone. They asked my name and told me I could fetch the—the—"

"Someone from the hospital here?"

"They said the Ullevaal Hospital, and then they told me Fru Hirschfeldt had no relations to collect the . . . body and that I should come to the hospital. So I came."

"But *who* told you?" She was thumbing through papers on the desk, looking for something. "If it was the hospital who telephoned to you I have had no notice of it here."

On the mantelpiece just to the right of the social worker was a clock with a pendulum made of three metal balls which spun round and back, instead of swinging back and forth. I could not keep my eyes off those spinning balls. They spun now, slowly to start, then faster . . . then slowing to stop, and starting back, and all the time there was a back-

ground of rustling papers and the occasional sniff from
the beaklike nose.

She lifted the telephone from its cradle. "I'll have to in-
quire."

"She is dead," I said pointlessly. "It is only to collect the
body."

The woman jogged at the cradle to attract the attention of the hospital exchange.

"You are a relation of the deceased?"

"A friend." I was thinking: *They will not let one who
is only a friend take the body away.* "Fru Hirschfeldt is
Jewish."

She gave me a keen look, then replaced the receiver. "I
see. Well—why didn't you say so at once instead of beating
about the bush? Some of you people have no intelligence."

"I only wished to collect the body, please. I was her
friend."

She stood up then, and possibly because I was nervous
she looked enormous. She terrified me by her sheer size.
When she stretched her arms after her long session at the
desk over the book she looked to me like a windmill. But
what she now said took all other thoughts from my head.

"I hope you have come soon enough. With these people
if no relatives come forward the bodies are used in the hospital for dissection. I'll telephone the mortuary for you."

This woman was clearly a Nazi sympathizer. To her it
meant nothing that Jewish bodies were cut up for dissection or otherwise disposed of. And a lot of trouble, too—
at this time of night. I was thinking then that Nils and his
workers should plan their schemes more carefully. They
should avoid people like this giantess with adenoids and

wristbones like doorknobs. To say nothing of an incipient goiter.

"What ward?" she suddenly flung at me in the middle of an exchange on the telephone. I could think of nothing to say, but suddenly logic came to my assistance.

"Sister Hjoerdis's ward." Surely Hjoerdis would have had Fru Hirschfeldt under her own care.

"She does not seem to be in the mortuary."

I knew then that I had to get out of the building while I could, before Hjoerdis got implicated, together with the others working with us. But how was I to get out?

"You will have to wait here in this room until I get the matter cleared up."

She was about to leave me to my fate when I thought that perhaps Nils and the others had, in fact, by-passed this dragon. Perhaps at the last moment they had not dared to risk an official removal of the body. Perhaps the man who answered the telephone in the mortuary—wherever it was—was one of us and was keeping his mouth shut. This was the rule that was always impressed on us, again and again. Better a thousand times to say nothing and rouse suspicion than to speak once too often and give something away. "There is always suspicion," Nils said. "A bit more or less won't hurt us much, but one indiscretion can sink the whole ship. Don't *talk*."

"The truck is at the mortuary," I said. "And here is my pass from the authorities to collect the body at this hour. It must be there, Sister."

That stopped the dragon. The police permit was something she could understand, and for some reason the fact that the truck was already there and waiting triggered a decision in that neolithic mind of hers.

"Well—no harm in your going down to see."

The balls were still spinning on the mantelpiece, but now I let them spin and got up. "Thank you, Sister. I shall manage."

"At this time of the night they wouldn't thank me for sending folk all over the hospital asking questions. Take the elevator at the end of the corridor."

"Thank you, Sister."

I found the elevator and pressed the bell. I craved to get away from the range of that woman with a passionate intensity. I thought that if I could get away everything would be all right with the world.

A huge elevator arrived and the doors opened. It was so big it could have held our truck. The attendant took me down without a word—down, down, and halt, in the half-darkness of the basement. A dark-eyed old man with an artificial leg met us there underground. He seemed very hostile and my hopes sank. I could see the slate slabs in the dim light and on them there were things under sheets . . . also long wooden boxes.

The old man took the form I had signed. "Who are you?" he demanded.

"Fru Astrup. Friend of the deceased."

"For the Jewess," he said, taking off his glasses. "All right. She's waiting for you. She won't run away."

I felt physically sick. He moved forward then and touched my hand. Then I knew this must be Hitchman, the Jewish Joessing, putting on an act.

"If you don't feel so good," he whispered, "go and sit

in the cab of the truck. It will be over in five minutes. You have done well. *Gud vaere med deg!*"

With his blessing ringing in my ears I went outside and waited in the truck. If this is bad for you, I thought again, what about poor Fru Hirschfeldt? I had not dared to look at the "boxes."

Eventually I heard the sound of a heavy box being pushed over wood into the back of the truck, and the driver came round and climbed up. We moved out of the hospital yard, past the policeman and the German soldiers. . . . We were on our way and Fru Hirschfeldt and Sara were safe in the back!

My thoughts went to her there, lying quietly with her daughter. They were probably wrapped in each other's arms, dreading—as I was—the sound of the engine slacking and the truck stopping to answer questions flung in harsh German. "You are bound to be stopped," Nils had said.

We drove down Kirkeveien, turned sharp left at Major-stuen into Bogstadveien, and no sound broke the night except the hum of the engine and the crunch of the freezing snow. Then on the corner of Holtegaten by Uranienborg Kirke a voice cried, *"Halte!"* The driver's expression did not change as he brought the truck to a standstill. A soldier opened the door and I saw that his rifle pointed up at us over the floor boards. The driver had a little book of papers ready which he casually handed to the German, who examined them with his flashlight. He handed the pass back and slammed the door without a glance at me.

The driver changed gears, down the hill and away toward our destination, which was somewhere near Grefsen.

This was all I knew. We had been traveling now about fourteen minutes and I knew that the journey should take twenty-five. We were halfway there and my job would soon be done.

"Halte!"—this time it was a German staff car. A lot of German troops were standing in the road by a garage, and we were surrounded.

A lieutenant questioned the driver, then said in German to him, "Get out." And almost immediately, "Get *out!*" he screamed. *"Schnell!"* The driver moved like a man shot from a gun. A Nazi pulled me out by the leg. German soldiers came out of the garage and began to climb into the back of the truck. The business was so sudden and so horrible I burst into tears, and this, strangely enough, was our salvation. . . .

It turned out that the lieutenant only wanted to get to some other place as quickly as possible. He had dismissed his transportation when he made a raid on the garage. Our driver told him that I was next of kin to a body which I was taking home for burial. The driver did not mention the word Jewess because—I now think—he would have been roughly treated for handling such a thing as a Jewish coffin.

The lieutenant turned to me and saluted. Like most Germans, he was very correct. *"Gnädige Frau,"* he said, "accept my regrets. I personally will see that you have your transportation back in half an hour at the most. I must move my men swiftly. I will leave you with a sergeant and two men to protect you. *Heil Hitler!"*

The coffin was lifted from the truck and placed on the ground in front of the pumps on the concrete of the garage yard. Silent beside it stood the sergeant and his two thugs.

The driver and I stood apart under the shelter, protected against the wind-driven snow. I was thinking of Fru Hirschfeldt and her little girl. If they moved! If the child cried out! I could not bear to think of it, but meanwhile I thought of the cold for them there under the drifting snow.

Once or twice, as we waited for the return of the truck, in absolute silence, the Germans turned to look at me. I did not like the way the sergeant was eying me. He had a pistol in his holster and we had all heard of what happened to girls who found a pistol held against them and a dark alley —or a garage—close at hand.

But the worst was yet to come—the thing that stood to betray us. After a while some sixth sense seemed to warn me that there was something wrong with the coffin. I stared in the half-darkness but could see nothing amiss. The district seemed empty of life. The gaping street stretched away into the darkness. Nothing was moving and somehow the impression came that we—the little group in the garage forecourt—were the only people in existence. I cannot explain the weird feeling. It was just there.

The scene is as clear in my memory today as it was when it happened. The forecourt of the garage was white with finely powdered snow which showed like a linen cloth in the thin light. Only our footsteps broke its glistening surface. Grouped by the pumps were figures like something unmoving out of a dream. No one spoke and no one moved. Then suddenly I saw that everything was white *except the coffin*.

I realized then what was wrong. The snow was melting as it fell on the wooden box. Around the coffin, too, was an edging clear of snow. The heat of the bodies in the coffin was betraying their presence. I pictured the two lying there, holding on to each other, terrified out of their wits by this sudden and unexpected hitch in their plans. I knew I had to do something before anyone noticed, but all I could do was to say rather stupidly, "I suppose the truck will be back soon and we shall be on our way again. It's cold."

I wanted Fru Hirschfeldt to hear and to be reassured.

The German sergeant turned his head to look at me. His face was not intelligent—but he was sharp enough, no doubt, to notice sooner or later that there was something warm and living inside the box. "You are ill?" he asked.

I expect I looked it, standing there shaking in every limb. "I do not feel well," I told him. "The cold—and the—"

"I understand. It was—a near relation?"

"My husband," I said. Then the idea came, suggested as is so often the case by what is actually happening around you at the moment. "I think I shall have to sit down." I stumbled over the snow and sat on the coffin itself. There was nowhere else to sit.

"It is bad to lose one's man," the German said. He offered me a cigarette and I took one from the packet and put it in my mouth with a hand that shook. The boy flicked a lighter, hiding the flame in his cupped hands because of the blackout. "That is better now, *nicht?*"

"Thank you," I answered. He stepped two paces back to where he had been standing with his companions, and silence fell over us again.

I cannot think of that scene even now without a shudder. There was nothing I could do but wait—wait for the scrunching of tires over the snow that would herald the return of the truck.

If only someone would move! If only I could do something! I saw the driven snow collect on the greatcoats of the Germans, emphasizing the folds and the surfaces against the wind. In times like this you tend to notice unimportant things.

And now suddenly, while I was watching the emptiness of the road outside the garage, I heard a soft sound in the snow and someone sat beside me on the coffin. "With your permission, *gnädige Frau*," a German voice said, and I feared its softness more than the command of the officer when he yelled at our driver to get down from his seat in the truck.

For a while I remained stiffly as I was, looking along the road. I was telling myself that this was how it started. If you are pleasant, that makes it easy—and conventional. Of course, if you are difficult, there is always the threat of the pistol.

I looked around and saw it was the sergeant. His eyes were moving over my hair—fair Nordic hair. He was looking as if searching for something. If I had ever known panic before, it was nothing like what this turned out to be in hard fact. I was not imagining this in the night when I knew I was really safe in bed. *This was happening.* Here on a wooden box in a snow-blown yard with no help near.

I looked for our driver. He was watching me neutrally. He did not seem interested, or alive to the danger. Maybe the other Germans would soon settle him if he tried to interfere.

"I thought you looked lonely and cold all by yourself, *gnädige Frau*," the sergeant said.

"I *am* cold," was all I could think of to answer him. Then an idea came to me that I suppose was essentially a woman's idea. I argued that if I made myself sympathetic, he would like me a little and I would have that amount of edge on the situation, anyway. "It was nice of you to come and sit by me." This made the business a gesture of courtesy, a masculine and chivalrous act of consideration.

The German moved closer to me, which made it all the better for an explanation of the melting snow—so I told myself. He was not bad-looking. He could not have been much more than twenty. Nevertheless, almost before I had time to think of what next to say, I found my hand in his hand, being gently rubbed.

"You will get frostbite, *gnädige Frau*. And that is not nice! Let me tell you that I was in Poland and there the hair freezes over your head if you take your cap off."

He was beginning to tell me about himself and to boast, which was all to the good and in the time-honored pattern of the male. But I wanted my hand back before he began to tell me I must not get frostbite in my shoulder, or perhaps around the waist. "You're not very blond for a good German," I teased him. "Let me see your hair. It won't freeze in Norway."

"Not as blond as you—but blond. See!" He shook his hair, which indeed was tow-colored and very thick, and grinned impudently. Then he replaced his cap.

"I would like another cigarette, please."

He took a cigarette and lit it for me, offering it to my lips with his fingers. It was a gesture of the night clubs and no doubt he was very proud of it. I saw that our driver was looking daggers at me now.

"*Gnädige Frau!* I would like to show you what we did to the pigs who own this garage."

"They—they were shot?"

"They were not here so we wrecked the place. They have been helping the Joessings so we stood and turnd our automatic weapons up and down the rows of cars. Come. I will show you."

Not for anything now would I have left that box. I clung to it as to a plank in a shipwreck. "I'm too cold to move," I said. "Not just now."

He sat for a while scuffing his heavy boots in the snow. "You should not live in a place like this. You should live in Germany. The world belongs to us now. In a few weeks we shall be in England. I shall be in London. I shall like that. They say the English girls are fair, like the Danes. I like the Danish girls."

I said to him, "I expect you like all the girls."

"Some," he admitted. His arm moved over the lid of the box and came up on the other side of my waist. It drew me closer to him. "*Herr Leutnant!*" I said, flattering his rank. "The others!"

"What do they count? *Gnädige—*"

"They count to me!"

"Well, come and I will show you what we did to those cars in the back."

I got up from the box. I had to, but I had no idea in my mind as to what I should do next. He was good-tempered and smiling now, but I knew all that could change in a flash. He was watching me expectantly.

"Well, *Fru Norsk?*"

I shook my head. Let him do what he wanted about my lack of sympathy, but let him do it here, out in the open. When I looked up his hand was on my arm and his eyes were different. They had a look that seemed to say I already belonged to him. "It is not always polite to refuse a well-meant invitation."

"It is not always possible to accept it, *Herr Leutnant.*"

I felt my arm jerked roughly as he came closer up behind me, but at that moment the sound of a car approaching reached the others and they began to move out into the road. One of the men called to the sergeant and I felt his hand drop away from my arm. The sensation of relief that came over me was actually like a wave. I felt it surge through me and then it drained away, taking the strength from my limbs. It is all very well to be strong and courageous in theory. Every woman has imagined situations like this, but living through one of them is a very different matter.

The truck swept into the garage and a corporal who was driving jumped out and saluted me. Speaking German, he gave me the officer's compliments, then they all helped to raise the coffin and slide it into the back. It was all I could do to climb back into the cab.

The corporal gave another smart salute—the German military salute with a snapping of the heels that always reminds me of the springing of a rattrap—and the sudden noise of it in the blanketing silence brought a little scream to my lips. The driver looked at me curiously. I said something but he did not answer as he shifted his gears and bumped out of the garage. We were on the road again, and away!

"Is it far?" I asked, but the driver stared, unresponsive, ahead. He was not impressed with the way I had been fraternizing with Nazis. But *he* did not know what was inside the coffin. We turned sharp right down a side street and the truck drove into a yard beside a big building. The driver switched off the engine and disappeared without a word to me. Soon I heard the scrape of the box being pulled out of the truck. I climbed down and a harsh voice said, "Get back!" Footsteps faded.

After a time the door opened and I saw the face of the driver. He stared at me with his face contorted into a sneer, then spat out, *"Din fordoemte Quisling!"* He slammed the door and *his* footsteps faded. I felt very cold and miserable as I waited.

Then: *"Kom, kjaere deg!"* a voice in the pitch-darkness said. I did not recognize it, but I climbed down and walked beside someone—a big man—until we reached the end of the yard. In the doorway Nils was waiting and he smiled down at me, saying, *"Du har vaert enestaaende!* You delivered them both safe and sound."

I tried to speak, but something in my throat prevented me. The nervous strain of the last hour had taken a toll of me and my legs were far from steady.

"There was some incident, I hear? What happened?"

I told him about being stopped by the patrol. I told him about sitting on the coffin and talking aloud to reassure Fru Hirschfeldt.

"She heard you and knew everything was going to be all right."

I was telling myself then that I wished I had had her faith. "Can I ask you something, Nils?"

"Of course!" He took my arm. "Don't worry about things so. You have done very well. Splendidly. Why shouldn't you ask me something?"

"I was told not to ask questions."

"You can always ask me questions. If I can't answer, I shall say so."

"Is—is *he* there?"

"All three. And they are going over the frontier into Sweden tomorrow. They have probably left here by now and everything's going to be all right for them. Don't worry! We're looking after them."

"I can't help thinking of poor Fru Hirschfeldt in—in the coffin, lying there with her arms around her little girl."

"Think of them in Sweden."

"Nils," I said. "It was the snow. The snow on the coffin. . . . It looked so bare with the plain wood showing and—"

"Think of them safe in Sweden."

I held on to his arm in silence until we got to the stopping place for the night streetcars. "What happens now?" I asked.

"I have a paper from the hospital giving us authority to be out at this hour," Nils told me. "We're relatives, if anyone wants to know. Not that anyone will."

"Nils," I said after a while, as the streetcar jogged along back toward the center of the town. "Are you going to tell that driver I'm not a Quisling?"

"He's not one of us. Don't trouble about him."

"I don't like him thinking the things of me that he must be thinking."

"Worrying again! What are you going to do now? Why don't you go away to Larkollen for a while?" Larkollen was where our country house was, on the fjord.

"In this weather?"

"At least you would only have the weather to worry about there. You would be quiet and away from it all, and Kirsti would enjoy not having to go to school. The food situation won't be so bad out there."

It was at this moment that a tall, elegant figure came back from the front part of the streetcar, and, seeing me, stopped. It was Jan Goffinger. He seemed very surprised to see me. He shot an inquiring look at Nils, who was staring stonily ahead, ready to know me or not as the situation suggested.

"You are out late, Helen," Jan said. There was a mild reproof in his voice—as if I had been out dancing and making merry!

"You too, Jan."

"Will you allow me to offer my company until you are safely back home?"

"I am already with a friend," I said. I put my hand on Nils's arm and he turned to acknowledge Jan. You never made introductions on public vehicles in Oslo while the Germans were there.

I could see that Jan did not like the look of Nils, who is no Adonis and who was in his workman's clothes, to make the situation more remarkable. But there was little Jan could say.

"Then I'll leave you here. *Adjoe,*" Jan said and got off the car. I watched him give Nils another look.

When I reached home Sister Hjoerdis was there waiting and with her were two nurses. Hjoerdis made me a sign to say nothing, and soon I was safe in my bed with a sleepy Kirsti tight in my arms. "I'm home," I told myself. "Safe and with Kirsti."

6

JAN COMES TO TEA

AT THIS PERIOD Jan Goffinger used to come to me twice a week for lessons in English, although frankly I have never been able to decide whether he really wanted to learn English for some special reason, or whether it was just a nice way of giving me some gold.

He was always on time to the split minute. His ring on the doorbell would mark the hour like a clock itself, and there he would be, stiff and formal, always well-dressed, with the tangy fragrance of lavender water about him. His suits were London-made and he had an Englishman's way of wearing them, quietly and in good taste. I liked Jan, I must confess; and knowing that I could depend on his punctual doorbell ringing and correctness was somehow very comforting.

Jan arrived at the apartment the day after I met him on the streetcar. It was not his "day" for a lesson, and as soon as I saw him outside our front door I knew something was not right. Jan was worried. Strangely enough for a Dutchman, he had that poker-faced, stiff, and formal manner generally to be associated with old-time Prussian officers, but now he looked rattled and uneasy. He left his hat and his stick and his gloves, as usual, in my hall—you could find them to the same half-inch in the dark at any time he was in the house—and for a while he stood at the window of our sitting room staring out over the snow. Then he turned and looked at me in rather a strange way before he said, "I am worried about you, Helen."

"About what?" Jan had what the Norwegians call an English mustache. That is to say he wore it clipped in a military way, and this made him look like a youngish general. His teeth were very white and there was a stern line to the shape of his cheekbones. He was not a talkative man, and the essential side of him, apart from his ferocious courage when roused, was—curiously enough—his shyness. It took months for Jan Goffinger even to begin to unbend with me.

"I do not think you should go about at night with the sort of man I saw you with last night."

I was about to blurt out that I had known Nils for years and that he was one of the best and most reliable of friends, and had been the same to my husband, but even with Jan I was cautious. I left it unsaid.

"Is—is anything wrong?"

"You should be careful with whom you associate. Particularly you. You are sure to be specially marked for observation by the Germans. You must realize that?"

"I realize I am Norwegian and that my husband was well-known. Everyone speaks well of him and the government—"

"Not this government, my dear." He paused and moved

over to my side. "Helen, you must be more practical. I know it is difficult for a woman to appreciate things in the way a man would view them. You must try. You must trust me. I advise you for the best—surely you know that?"

"Of course I do, Jan! I don't know what I should do without you. So cheer up! If I have done anything stupid, I promise I won't do it again."

He smiled his stiff smile then, and I thought that in all the time I had known him I could not recall a joke he had made or a situation he had found humorous.

"I'm going to make tea and you can put the kettle on for me."

He came with me into the kitchen and stood watching me, and again womanly instinct told me something was very much out of the ordinary here. Whenever I have had that sort of "warning feeling," it has always been right. I am not one of those women who laugh at such things, for there are times when you know something is wrong without any room for doubt; but how you know, or why you know, is—quite illogically—in itself unknown.

I concentrated on making lime tea in my best Queen Anne silver pot. Like my china, this was English, and I knew Jan appreciated such things—which Nils certainly did *not*. Nils would be happier drinking tea strong enough to stain the teeth, out of a mug you could use as a missile if the occasion arose.

I first met Jan Goffinger at a party in Gulleraasveien before the war. When he heard my broken Norwegian—then worse even than his own—he asked me very diffidently what nationality I was, and I told him I had been born English. At that, for the rest of the evening he never let me out of his sight, although he did not speak to me again. I remember that at the time I thought what a manly type he looked—something very handsome and like an eagle. You felt he could be an awkward customer on occasion among men, but he would always be kind and considerate to women.

Then I lost track of him until soon after my husband was lost. By then he had taken a furnished apartment in Schultzgate and was living there with his widowed cousin. The fact that she had been widowed only the previous month by the death of her officer-husband in Poland—I never knew which side he was on—made a link. Jan called on me formally and politely, first with his cousin, then alone, and told me he wished to see as much of me as I would so kindly allow because during a ten months' stay in London, where he had lived near Kensington Gardens in a garage apartment, he had learned English and did not wish to "lose" it. Would I converse with him in English?

I was only too glad to have someone to talk to, but not much of our talk turned out to be in English, for, indeed, he knew very little beyond what would get him a meal in a London restaurant or a ride to approximately where he wished to go on the underground. I can still hear him asking, "You wasn't tser, vas you?" when he wanted to know if I had been in London at the time he was there. Anyway, the lessons began.

Soon after, one Sunday, he called and took Kirsti and me out on an excursion he had planned. We went to the railway station and took *holmenkollbanen* to Slemdal, from where we walked through the forest to Midstuen and up the hills to Frognersaeteren. From this height you can look out right over Oslo and far out into the Oslo Fjorden. On a clear, sunny day—and this was—it is a view you can never forget; although I have seen it many times, each time it strikes me anew. Jan showed it to me as if he had some interest in it from a personal angle.

Whilst Kirsti was skipping about amusing herself he told me a good deal about himself and his early life. It was a very happy day for me and I think my own contented frame of mind managed in some way to infect him, too. The war seemed far away. It was not often one could relax, and that afternoon I felt for once that I could throw off all cares and troubles—and I did. Jan told me he had never married because he had never met anyone like his mother. I think that should show the state of mind we had arrived at!

When a man gets to this stage he has to be taken seriously, for it usually means he has been giving a good deal of private thought to the person in whom he suddenly finds himself confiding. And when any one person is much in another's private thoughts it means you have a niche there for yourself. You have to be careful not to tumble yourself out of it, however precariously and for whatever silly reason he has managed to perch you there.

From his conversation Jan appeared very attached to his cousin. She was a striking girl, like himself dark-eyed and raven-haired. Jan, who was in his early forties, was touched with gray at the temples, and the corners of his eyes wrinkled into tiny, hairlike cracks when he smiled. "Good-nature marks" the Norwegians call them. The cousin was about twenty-eight and of course free of gray hairs, as yet. Otherwise, she looked like him. Jan told me that he was taking care of her, as she had been left ill-provided for by her late husband, who had certainly never expected to make a premature exit at the age of thirty-two. She wanted to stop in Oslo for the war as she thought it safer, and Jan had humored her whim. They both had money in Spain, and Jan had money, too, in Rio—so he told me. Before the war actually broke out he had spread his capital in Switzerland, South America, and for some reason, Spain. I gathered he must have a considerable fortune from what he said, but he actually gave me no direct hint. I never for a moment imagined he had anything like the sum I was later to find out he had with him in Oslo.

Jan promised to take his cousin anywhere she wanted to go—America, South Africa, Australia. He wanted to get her mind off her husband. From what he told me that afternoon I gathered that she had been with him in London before the war, and that they had also traveled all over Switzerland together. I was to realize later why Jan had been telling me about his finances and his hopes and—in the shape of his cousin—his encumbrances. I did not give it a thought at the time. I was far too happy and carefree to search for causes.

In fact, I was thinking chiefly of how kind Jan had always been to me. When the Germans came to Oslo he had helped me in a hundred ways. On April 10 the Norwegian wireless gave out an official announcement—through the Quislings, of course—that the town must be evacuated by 2:00 P.M. The government could take no responsibility for anyone left behind, they said, because a heavy attack by air from English bombers was due at 2:00 P.M. Soon everyone was talking of the six hundred RAF planes that were coming to wipe the town out. . . . I have never known such panic! Women were to be seen sitting about everywhere, weeping. Whole families rushed like folk deranged, getting their cars and all the gas they could obtain, tearing around to the banks for valuables to carry off from the doomed city, clutching their children to them! The Norwegians are a people most would admit as courageous. Their history is one of determination, steadfastness, and a fine sort of unemotional courage. No one would have dreamed it that day seeing what was going on in Oslo!

I must admit I was infected by the panic. Remember, this was a government announcement made over the radio to the nation. "Leave the town at once!" we were ordered. "The town is about to be destroyed from the air by the British." So naturally enough, I prepared to leave. I packed three suitcases with food—far too much to carry when we tried to leave the apartment. I discarded two, and repacked one with which I could manage to walk about fifty yards at a time before changing hands. Kirsti had a little rucksack.

Outside in the street, people were standing in front of cars as they came along, begging for rides to get them out of the doomed city before they were killed. Some of the cars were so loaded you could hardly see them for people clinging on like flies. I saw at once that it was hopeless to try to get a lift and time now was getting close. I took Kirsti back to the block. The place was empty now. Not a soul was to be seen anywhere. Front doors were left open, luggage was spilled in the hall, suitcases and bags were lying about, discarded in the rush. Some unthinking tenants had even left dogs and cats behind.

In our hall of entrance—there were several entrances to the block, each with its elevator—we heard a canary singing its heart out, and Kirsti discovered it in a cage lying on its side where it had rolled behind the stairway. Someone had dropped the cage and made a run after some car. We picked "Billy" up and carried him back to our flat. We never found out to whom he belonged and Kirsti adopted him, giving him the rather silly name of "Billy" out of her own head on the spur of the moment.*

"Kirsti," I said, "the English do not bomb women and children. You know they wouldn't do that, don't you?"

"Yes, Mummy," she answered, but she would have said yes to anything. I was thankful that she was occupied with the canary, for now that I was back in the flat I was terrified. I knew we were going to be caught by the bombers and were going to be killed by our own folk. I no longer thought then of Norway as my home. I did not want to die in a far country and even more I did not want my little girl to be killed without ever seeing England.

The whole town seemed utterly silent. I told myself that they had all gone. In the whole of Oslo, I thought, there were only us two! It is a terrible, desolate feeling when you have to admit the fact that all the herd has passed on and left you alone to face what is coming. I admit frankly that I was so afraid as time went silently on, with the minutes steadily ticking off the hour when the English bombers would come to destroy us, that I became distracted. All

* We still have Master Billy and he still sings his heart out here in the middle of London with the buses rumbling down Sloane Street beneath the balcony where his cage stands on fine days!

sorts of silly thoughts came into my head. All kinds of ridiculous plans.

I knew that Kirsti would soon see how terrified I was, so I went into the bedroom, leaving her with the little bird, and in a strange way, without actually willing it, I found myself saying my prayers. I do not know what I prayed for, but I was there half-sprawled over my bed for a long time —in fact, until I was called out of whatever state I had fallen into by the sound of Kirsti repeating my name in an anxious voice.

I walked out of the room feeling very different. It may have been the relief to my feelings of allowing myself to give way at last, but I felt like another woman from that time on. "Well, you see, darling," I said, "they haven't destroyed us yet and it's ten past two!"

This was not so, but I wanted to say something to cheer Kirsti up. She, too, could feel the extraordinary tension created by the absolute stillness of the city. The streetcars were not running; there were no trains; everything had ceased as the people took to the hills.

When the front doorbell rang I screamed, and Kirsti ran to hug me around the knees. We both stood there, not making a sound, and after an age the bell sounded again. I was expecting it this time, and managed to stifle a squeak.

"You should not scream, Mummy," Kirsti told me gravely. "The English bombers will know we are here."

"The English bombers are airplanes, dear," I told her, "and this is someone at the door."

The bell rang again and now I could hear someone calling, "Helen! Helen!" I opened the door to Jan, who merely removed his hat and his gloves and placed them as usual with his stick precisely in their accustomed place on the table in the hall.

"I had to walk every step of the way to get here," he said. "I knew you would not panic and go. I would have phoned but the girls at the exchange were the first to leave. I tried to telephone to you as soon as I heard the announcement, but my line was dead by then. What a spectacle!"

"You shouldn't have come here," I said stupidly. "A big block of apartments like this they would destroy first." I believed this—passionately—absurd though it now seems! In times of panic the weirdest ideas seem logical.

"My dear," Jan said, "control yourself. There isn't going to be an air raid! The Quislings wanted to scare everyone into hating England. And now they have succeeded! Since that broadcast they have been trying to get the people back to their posts—the streetcar conductors and the trainmen and the telegraphists and the dustmen."

"You mean there isn't going to be bombing? They're not going to destroy the town?"

"The RAF don't have six hundred bombers, and they couldn't send them here if they had. Besides who wants to destroy Oslo? Certainly not the British!"

"But everyone has left!"

"The first touch of war on the nation. It always brings panic, but later the people settle down. In time, if taken by degrees, they will get used to anything. It is the first touch that throws the panic. They'll all come back—wiser and angrier. It was a shrewd move by someone."

"I can't believe it's—it's not going to happen after all."

"Just wait and see then, my dear." He turned to look at the canary. "What is this?"

I explained to him, and he said we should not have brought the bird in with us. "You have enough to look after in your daughter," he said.

An odd streak in his character left him unmoved by cruelty to animals. The fact of the bird having been dropped and left to die meant nothing to him—weren't there millions of birds in the world with literally hundreds dying every minute? This is logical but it is not humane, and I for one am very glad we took care of Billy as we did.

Outside the window we could see that our *vaktmester* had not deserted. He was filling sacks with sand and dragging them against the walls of the house. He was working slowly and patiently on—a true Norwegian, not giving a tinker's damn what came at him from the air, or from anywhere else, for that matter. I made tea, and somehow before I realized it, it was after four o'clock. Jan stayed with us until the next day. I tucked Kirsti up in her bed early that evening, but Jan and I stayed awake all night watching the people streaming back into the town. Some friends from the apartment on the floor above had gone in their car as far as Hoenefoss, taking their silver and their jewelry with them in a trunk. They broke down and had to abandon everything and walk. They arrived back in Oslo without their car and without their valuables and they never saw either again. Some went so far they did not get back for a week!

Now here it was almost a year later, and here was Jan paying an unexpected visit, and I was making him tea again, with my best Queen Anne pot and best tea set, and dodging the issue about being seen after curfew.

I carried the lime tea into the sitting room, where Billy,

the canary, was singing. Jan was too preoccupied to notice. He did not seem to be able to sit for long, and soon he was at his favorite position in the window, his cup in his hand as he looked toward Holmenkollbakken. Often when he visited me he would stand at the window and then call me to his side when he spied Kirsti and her friends come frisking around the corner from school, their satchels flying in the air, before they assembled like a flight of starlings at our entrance to make their farewells until the next day. There were two girls from the same school living in our block. Fru Hirschfeldt's little girl used to make another of them.

But this afternoon there was some time yet before we could expect Kirsti back when Jan suddenly turned around with the queerest look on his face. "I came around here from our flat in Schultzgate, Helen, to—to see you this afternoon."

As this seemed fairly obvious I made no reply. He put his cup down away from the edge of the table, where it could not be knocked off. "I wanted to talk to you. I have something to say that may not please you." He waited. "There comes a time when everyone must stop whatever he is thinking about at the moment and step outside of himself and reflect where all this is heading."

He took two quick steps—as if he had been suddenly pushed in the middle of the back—and took my hand in his.

"Helen, I must ask you—" he began, when the noise of a key in the front door stopped him. It was surely Jan's unlucky day, for Kirsti came in, bursting with news.

"Something has gone wrong with the heating at school!

No more wood!" she exulted. "They had to send us all home and we can't go tomorrow! Hello, Uncle Jan!"

You would have thought the war had ended! Then Kirsti stopped and looked at Jan. "You've shaved your mustache to look like Hitler's!" she said, and I saw that this was true. This was not the first time I had occasion to notice how observant children are. "No one will think you are a Dutchman now. They will think you are a German and you won't be able to get any cigarettes in the shops!"

"Then I shall have to grow my mustache again," Jan said.

"I liked you better with the old one."

"Kirsti!" I said.

"Look, dear," Jan said in a queer sort of voice for him, for he was generally so good with children. "I have something to say to your mother, so just run along for a minute like a good little girl."

Kirsti nodded and walked obediently toward the kitchen, but I knew as soon as she had closed the door her eye would be glued to the keyhole. I knew that demure look.

"Helen," Jan said. "All the time I am away from you, Helen. . . . I mean, this panic and danger—it has made me realize that I am always thinking of you. You are always in my thoughts. Will you marry me?"

For a man so attractive, he was very gauche, almost naïve. His shyness had prevented him having much experience with women, but that is often the type who can give the biggest surprises. For once, this was truly *so* sudden. What was there to say? To be sincere I should, of course, have asked him, "What on earth has got into your head to make you suddenly decide you want to marry me?"

But no woman ever asks that honest question because it is, to say the least, not flattering.

"I have never thought of you in that way," I told him, which was less than a half-truth. Nine women out of ten would think like that about him in the first ten seconds.

"I do not want to press you for an answer now, so say nothing until you have thought about it. Do not be hasty. You must have known how I felt for a long time."

"I don't need to think about anything. The answer is no. I have Kirsti to think about. And I like you much more as a friend."

He took hold of my arm and from the way he held on against my feeble—and more or less conventional—attempts to release it, you might have thought that the answer to his plea depended on the maintenance of some form of jujitsu grip between us.

"I have no time for men. Kirsti is my whole life and I am content."

"You are very young still. And so attractive. You must be attractive to all men, but to me, Helen—"

"This is rather undignified," I said. At the back of my mind was a little face glued to the keyhole taking all this in with photographic accuracy. "Please, Jan! Please get up from your knee!"

It had never occurred to me that any man would have the idea that an impassioned appeal made literally at one's feet still passed muster, but I must admit that I now saw how in the old days such an approach was *de rigueur*. It can be rather touching. In Jan it was only silly, although there was truly a suggestion of the laying of a heart at your feet, which is the sort of thing that appeals to a woman in a sentimental moment.

"Then you will give me my answer tomorrow morning?"

"Yes, yes."

His face relaxed, and a wintry smile came. "Now I can ask you something which your answer one way or another would have compromised. Sit down, my dear, and listen carefully."

He had already asked me to marry him, and I wondered what could be coming next. Before I sat down I walked to the door, but, of course, by the time I got there Kirsti was in the kitchen innocently pouring herself out her tiny ration of milk, obtained through Jan. "It's all over for now," I said. "One day you'll get a cold in your eye and it will serve you right. But I'm going to lock you in here for a few minutes while Mr. Goffinger talks business with me."

I locked the kitchen door and returned to the sitting room. "Well?"

"You know that I have a little gold here in Oslo. I have been collecting it since before the war to be safe, and how right I was. But lately I have not been easy in my mind. These Quislings know too much. Their police work is excellent and they are quite ruthless in their methods and their aims."

"I know," I said. Many people turned their money into gold at the start of the war only to find that gold is easily stolen unless kept in strong rooms, and, when stolen, easily changed into something without any history or identity.

"I want to hide what I have. I want somewhere altogether unconnected with me or with anywhere I have frequented. I have a favor to ask."

"You can ask me anything."

"Your house at Larkollen on the fjord. I want to take the gold secretly out of Oslo. I have a boat I could use and not a soul would know. You and I and Erik."

"Who is he?"

"He is a friend. An old servant. He is steady and loyal but too big a fool to gossip. It is all quite watertight, I assure you, and no one would ever think of looking in the cellars of your house in Larkollen. We could bury it on the place, if it came to that. There is nothing to connect me with Larkollen, and it is so remote. Didn't you say that you cannot get there by road in winter, or at least with difficulty?"

"No one in his right mind would think of living there in the winter. The drifts sometimes come up to the bedroom windows and there is no way of getting deliveries of anything at all until the longer days and the spring."

"Would you let me hide the gold there?"

"Of course!"

"And help us?"

"Of course! Any time!"

Jan took my hand and gently squeezed it. "You are so lovely," he told me, as if it were really so. "I would sooner rely on you than on many men I know. The time of these long nights helps. I will tell you of my plans, if I may?"

After Jan left me, I let my daughter out. I would not tell her what had been going on and this made her sulk a little, but I was really too embarrassed, not by the promise I had made to help him, but by his sudden proposal of marriage. A man of his type does not give way to impulse. He must

have been thinking of asking me to marry him for weeks—
if not months.

The gist of the matter about the gold was that he wanted
me to go down to the harbor to look at the cabin cruiser he
had managed to get hold of, for he insisted that I would
know something about ships, having been married to a
seafaring man. In fact, I know very little about sailing and
less about engines, but I can pull my weight as deckhand
and am never seasick. I had been over a good deal of salt
water about the fjords, of course, but this did not make me
competent to judge the seaworthiness of any craft. Jan insisted on secrecy and discretion. He told me where the boat
lay, described her lines, and gave me her name, *Leonora*.
I would not be able to go aboard and look her over, but he
wanted me to stroll past once or twice, taking in her lines so
that I could easily recognize her again, if that turned out to
be necessary before we sailed. Above all, I was not to attract
attention or to do anything that might connect me with the
craft in any way.

This I promised to do.

7

CURIOSITY KILLED

SOMETHING HAPPENED in our block of apartments, however, that put the thought of the *Leonora* out of mind for a while. It was something which really made me face up to what the Resistance meant and what working with the Joessings involved. I think it was Sverre's part in it which brought it home to me the most. He was such a nice boy, quiet and full of fun. He was a medical student and I think he had the nicest manners of any youth I have ever known. If ever I have a son of my own I would like him to grow up to resemble Sverre.

It started, as usual, with Nils, who came to my place after everyone had gone to bed, in defiance of the curfew and with the connivance of our *vaktmester,* who, I believe, used to stand in the shadows of his doorway in the courtyard keeping watch all the time Nils was inside the building. Nils came up the drainpipe of my balcony and sat on my bed. I was no longer frightened at this procedure. I never had the habit of locking my bedroom door, because of Kirsti; and now I wouldn't have been allowed to had I wished. But with it all, I had a feeling that I was no longer a defenseless woman on her own, since at any time of the night I might find Nils shaking my shoulder and sitting on my bed. It may sound illogical, but I am sure anyone who has lived for any length of time under an ever-present fear will understand what I mean. You fear that someone one night will come. That is your obsession. Then someone, in fact, does come, and it turns out to be your best friend and your protector, so in time you lose the fear of someone coming in the night.

Nils told me he had been sent to see me because our group wanted the use of my apartment. They were going to make a raid on the apartment of a wealthy Quisling, an accountant in an influential position, who lived on the next staircase to ours. This man was thought to have possession of a list of names we wanted to suppress. My windows formed an ideal watching place for the raid; in addition, the three men who were to undertake the actual work were to start out from my apartment, where they could spend some time previous to the sortie in hiding.

"Won't they know they came from here?" I asked.

"Of course not," Nils said. "We have everything planned to the last move and no one will ever know how it happened. Not even Bugge himself."

Nils, in his job as a refrigerator serviceman, spent his business hours going from apartment to apartment in the best quarters of the town taking down complaints and putting small mechanical matters right. His knowledge of our part of Oslo, in particular, was certainly unrivaled. (His joke was that he would have made an excellent burglar.)

This was of the greatest help to our group. Nils had a good excuse if found almost anywhere.

In some way Nils had discovered that Bugge had compiled a very dangerous list together with damaging information about the Joessings. The list of suspects was, in fact, very accurate. He had included information about the occupations of his suspects and the reasons for his suspicion of them. Nils had actually seen some of this material himself—how, I never knew—and he wanted to get hold of it. However, he did not tell me that night that they were going to kill Bugge when his wife left to go to tea with a friend of hers, as they knew she planned to do.

Why people like Bugge went to such lengths to work against the patriots is difficult to say, but we had several like him in the building, especially *Arkitekt* Hagen, an old woman of a man who could not keep his sharp nose out of things. Perhaps they honestly thought the salvation of Norway was in the German way of life. Perhaps they thought of us and King Haakon as the real traitors to Norway. Perhaps they just wanted to advance themselves.

After Nils had told me what to do, he disappeared, and in half an hour came back to my bedside. It was then a quarter past four in the morning. "They're in the kitchen," he said. "When you get up they will go to bed. Don't let Kirsti know."

"Who are they?" I asked. "Are they to be trusted?"

It was then he gave me the name of Sverre, whom I knew well. The other two I did not know. They were boys of twenty, Joergen and Oscar. You could have searched Oslo for two more different types, for Joergen was a dockhand and small and tense and very powerful, while Oscar was tall and languid with aristocratic connections both in Norway and in England, and, but for the war, would have been at Oxford where he had some sort of traveling scholarship at Christ Church.

After Nils left, I could no longer sleep, so I got up and, warning the others not to wake Kirsti—who has very sharp ears, especially for anything she is not supposed to hear— I made them some German cocoa.

What they had to do later that day did not seem to worry them at all, which would have surprised me even more had I known that Sverre was picked to kill Bugge with a knife. They had to work without noise and using to the full the element of surprise. But of course they were not allowed to tell me anything; we spoke of other things while they had their cocoa, then I put them into my bedroom and locked the door. Sverre said he would see that no one snored.

I watched the sky get lighter from my windows, until I could decently wake my daughter, then I fixed her breakfast and packed her off to the house of a little friend of hers for the day. You will remember there was no school because there was no wood for heating. In fact, the situation soon afterward became so bad that for weeks their class at school was held from day to day in the house of any parents that happened to have fuel.

Nils had found out that Bugge kept his list in the bank in safety, but that this day he had removed it from the strong room to take round to headquarters. Today the papers for once would be in his room, in his desk, and Nils planned to get them before Bugge took them to a security meeting he was called to attend that night at the Victoria Terrasse.

I was quite alone in the apartment at 3:50 that afternoon when my guests came out of the bedroom, where they had slept all day unseen and unheard, and let themselves quietly out of my front door. They walked down instead of taking the elevator, and our *vaktmester* led them into the interior courtyard. This they crossed, dodging in and out among the cords of wood, stacked ten feet high—the fuel reserves of our buildings—and entered the archway giving on the stairway on which the Bugges lived.

My job was to watch from my window and make a signal with a red cloth to a car parked down the street if anything went wrong. All I had to do was watch, and if an alarm was raised inside the building I was to stand at the window and slowly wave the red cloth until the car had disappeared.

I immediately went to my window to watch, and almost at once I saw the red-headed Joergen stroll out on the street side of the building and lounge at the entrance. This I think was a mistake. I know that people like Nils who plan these things have been through dozens of such raids themselves and know more than I could ever know, but I speak only of facts when I say that I noticed Joergen at once. In his rough clothes he looked out of place in our block. He looked in himself suspicious, and in addition he was lolling about without any apparent excuse to be there. If they had chosen, say, Sverre, and given him a nice-looking girl to be talking to, no one would have bothered. All the world likes a lover, and who wouldn't linger to talk to a pretty girl?

Fru Bugge came out next and walked down the pavement directly below the window. I would have liked to push a flowerpot onto her head for she was a very unpleasant person in her own right, in addition to being the wife of a selfish man like Bugge, whose long spying watches and the lists he made were aimed at winning him official favor.

Arkitekt Hagen, another Quisling, whose apartment was on the other side of ours farther down the street, was a strange character. He was as curious as a cat. He could never resist taking a look out of his window to see what was going on, particularly if one of the neighbors happened to be leaving her apartment or, better still, returning to it with some strange man. *Arkitekt* Hagen was one of the cleverest architects in Oslo, but when at home he was always looking out of his windows. This afternoon he happened by chance to be home. And being home he was looking out of the window. I noticed him when I was watching Fru Bugge pass, myself unseen. At the time I thought nothing of it.

But when I looked again I saw that the architect was watching Joergen.

I thought: If Nils were here he could warn them. He could do something to get Joergen out of sight. But I could not leave my post. It had been impressed on me that each had to do exactly what he or she was ordered, and nothing else. We worked on the assumption that everything had been thought of and each had to do his little part and forget the rest. I stayed on at the window, and not for a moment did the architect take his eyes off the unlucky Joergen. To make matters worse, Joergen kept alternately staring anxiously down the street—where he anticipated the trouble would come from if it came—and then glancing swiftly up at the Bugges's windows. Anyone watching was bound to know something was going on.

Suddenly I saw the architect turn sharply on his heel and disappear. I thought he might be telephoning to the police, so I risked everything and slipped down the stairs to the *vaktmester,* whom I found at the furnace below ground. When I told him what I had seen, he sent me back to our apartment at once. "I'll get them away," he said. "Don't let anyone see you about. There are enough in this already. Go! Go now!"

I crept upstairs again. No one, I am sure, saw me. I was without a hat and in light house shoes, and I would have had a job to explain what I was doing. But I was lucky and got back to the apartment without meeting a soul. Joergen was still outside the building keeping watch. There was no sign of *Arkitekt* Hagen. I hoped Nils would not be severe with me for raising a false alarm. I began to breathe anew.

Then the police cars arrived. There were three of them and they came full speed up to the block to brake suddenly and swerve into the curb. Almost before they had stopped the men were in the street, dividing on some prearranged plan. Joergen had disappeared, where and when I do not know, for by then I was obeying my orders and waving the cloth to and fro. I did not wave for long, as the little car left almost at once and went off quite leisurely down the street.

Some of the police went through to the back of the block and posted themselves with their automatic rifles among the woodpiles. That cut off the back. There were men on our stairs, both back and front, and men in the block on the other side. Even I knew then that the three boys were cut off from escape. In front of the house there were at least a dozen armed police watching the roof and all the windows. Strangely enough, after the first rush there was a long time of utter silence when nothing seemed to be happening. I saw the postman enter the building higher up the road, flicking over the letters from his bag as he always did; and there was even a cat on one of the balconies with her back leg straight up in the air while she screwed her head around to perform her toilet.

I stood by the window, out of sight, as ordered, praying that everything would come all right, reassuring myself that *Arkitekt* Hagen had not known which apartment they were in. I hoped that Joergen had got clear before the place was circled. Then a burst of automatic rifle fire came, followed by two sharp reports. This was the end of Joergen. When the police arrived he tried to warn the others by rushing up to the flat. Halfway up the stairs, he met Sverre and Oscar racing down.

"The woodpiles," Sverre ordered briefly. He was in charge and he had heard the police cars, which were even then pulling up at the street entrance.

The three men separated at the back—the exit to the courtyard. It was too late for them to get out, but they did not realize it. The police in our doorway caught sight of Joergen as he dodged from stack to stack in a desperate attempt to get safely across the yard and make his escape on the far side. The burst of automatic fire took the right-hand side of his head away and he died as he dropped among the stacked wood.

The two following reports were from Sverre's Luger automatic pistol, a very powerful German weapon which had been stolen from the Gestapo. Sverre killed two of the police on our stairs with those two lucky shots. He was immediately shot in the back and killed on a balcony overlooking the yard on the second floor.

How Oscar escaped was a miracle. I simply did not see him at all. He was in that courtyard, first among the wood-piles, and later crouched under some bicycles in a shed, for nearly an hour while police searched for him. They never found him. He kept moving all the time, and got away in the little car I had been signaling, which had gone off to wait in a prearranged rendezvous nearby.

The police found the body of Henrik Bugge almost at once, the back of his head crushed like an egg and a knife in him. They unluckily found most of the papers too, for the men did not have time to collect them all, and the Germans knew then how important these papers must be to the Resistance movement, and so could judge of the accuracy of their information.

It was horrible seeing the bodies of those young men, who only a few hours earlier had been laughing and joking and sleeping on my bed. I had no idea there was so much blood in the world. And it made things no easier for me to hear, day after day, from the *vaktmester's* wife of the state of Fru Bugge's Kirzhan carpet of which she was so proud. It was soaked through and through, she kept insisting, and where it had dried a little, it was stuck to the floor, so that they had first to get it free with a bread knife slid under-neath. Some people gloat over details like this.

Before the police left the building, they searched every apartment and questioned everyone, but thanks to Nils and his staffwork I had nothing to fear. No one had had a chance to see anything as far as my apartment was con-cerned. No one would have noticed anything at all if it had not been for the piece of bad luck that made *Arkitekt* Hagen decide to return home that afternoon.

8

IN ALL INNOCENCE

THE SNOW had stopped and the sun was shining over the town the afternoon I went down to Maritim, the basin where, in the days before the Germans came, the wealthier residents of Oslo kept their yachts. I went by streetcar, getting off at the stopping place at Skoeyen, and as I walked down under the railway bridge and looked over the slowly moving river I could not help thinking of the old days and how little one then suspected life could suddenly become so complicated and uneasy.

The little harbor was still crowded with small craft, most of them laid up with their canvas covers lashed tightly over them like grotesque pots of preserve as they lay side by side at the moorings. Coils of loosely rolled barbed wire trailed along the quayside, leaving only a gap beside the temporary guardhouse that had been erected by the Germans—a kind of large telephone booth. This structure made the place look like a customs post, yet there was a deserted, rather sinister air about the harbor that once had been so gay with white paint and sails against the sparkle of the sun on the water.

Norwegian *statspoliti* were patrolling out toward the breakwater and back, while their comrade stood with his rifle at the telephone booth staring out over the water. Beyond, out in the fjord, you could see the gray shapes of German warships. I knew then that Jan had been right in telling me not to linger. I walked quickly toward the café on the corner, as if I had business in the neighborhood, and saw the *Leonora* at once.

There was no mistaking her lines. She looked a lovely boat to me. As I subsequently learned, she was about twenty-eight feet on the water line, broad in the beam, with a cruiser stern and a cockpit forward. She had a single cabin amidships and the engines aft, with twin screws, and ran on Scottish-built gasoline engines made by Ailsa Craig. The steering was operated behind a large curved glass windshield, after the fashion of a car. She was double-skinned, Oslo-built, and nothing if not seaworthy, and her powerful engines gave her an actual speed in average sea conditions of eighteen knots, reputed twenty. But her consumption at that speed would be very high. She carried fuel tanks for three hundred gallons!

I did not like to walk back again along the quay, so I turned on the corner by the café into a side street. A big man in a peaked seaman's cap was standing by the café door and it was obvious that he was not sober. I do not know what impressed him so keenly on my mind. Perhaps I was keyed up and receptive. He was a Dutch type, blond and heavy-built, with a straggling mustache stained by tobacco smoke, and he seemed to be staring at me in a muddled sort of way. When Jan later questioned me and asked in particular if anyone had noticed me down there on the quay at Maritim, the only person I described was this big Dutchman who was drunk.

Jan came round to see me that same evening, for he was getting anxious about his plans. I had by then already explained to him, and convinced him, that I did not wish to get married again to him or to anyone, and he took it very well. He told me more about the gold that night.

"Whenever you have gold you have danger. Anywhere in the world the same rule applies. There are many more valuable things, but gold has always represented something among men that nothing else ever has. I have enough of it to make trouble, so do not think I am being overcautious."

He wanted me to travel unobtrusively down to Maritim the next evening, well muffled up for a sea trip. I would be met at the wire where the sentry was. A dinghy would be waiting to take me aboard. I was to say nothing and do nothing, and when aboard the *Leonora* just wait.

"I have several cases to get aboard. It is better for you to know nothing about it," Jan said. "Don't be late, or fail us in any other way. Everything has been very carefully planned and one little hitch would put the whole operation out of gear."

I thought, in spite of his warning, that he was being overdramatic. "How shall I recognize who is to pick me up?"

"There is not likely to be more than one dinghy waiting at the steps. It may be me, or Erik, or another you will meet—a Norwegian called Birger. He has been in your

Navy. We have to have him to navigate. He knows this coast like the back of his hand."

"There was only one gap in the wire and beside it was the sentry box."

"That all has been taken care of."

My trust in Jan must have been complete, for I did not worry about the trip; in fact, I was looking forward to it more than a little. I had the urge to get away for a while from Oslo—even from Kirsti. It was one of those moods. Here was a call to get moving and I was more than ready to go. I spent next morning preparing a warm outfit of slacks and sweater with my old sea boots and thick stockings. It can be cold in the fjords when the wind is off the mountains, and at this time of the year we had a very short day and long hours of darkness. I then took Kirsti off in a streetcar to the house of a friend where she would be staying for the few days I expected to be away. She parted from me, as is the way of the young, without even a second look, so engrossed was she with a little friend who—among other marvels—had a child's bicycle which it was Kirsti's overwhelming ambition to ride.

Back alone in the apartment, I packed a canvas bag and there I was, all ready for the trip hours too soon. To while away the time I wrote a good deal in my diary, for which I had a special hiding place, then when the hour at length came I left the place just as it was and slipped down to the *vaktmester* to ask his help in leaving the block by the back way through the wood-stacked courtyard, unobserved.

I was sharply surprised to find Nils with old Pettersen. They were down in the boiler room, a place which had the advantage of several exits while being close to the cellars.

I did not know it then, but this was a place our group often used for meetings and discussions. Nils was hearing all about the tragedy of Sverre and Joergen. He told me I had done right, even in leaving my post to warn Pettersen, and further, the *vaktmester* had told Nils what I had had to say about a man like Joergen being posted in the street. I don't think we ever made that particular mistake again.

Nils himself was surprised to see me, dressed as I was in old slacks and a raincoat that had seen good service. He had the right to ask where I was going, for I might have been given some small job to do of which he had not been told. I evaded his question, however. I merely said I was going out to see if I could get food.

I had the thought then that I should confide in Nils. He was a great source of strength at all times. But I did not tell him. There was no particular reason why I should have concealed my real intentions except that to cover up was by then almost second nature. Also Jan had rather scared me with his tales of what men will do under the lure of gold. But from this time of seeing Nils and excluding him from my plans I began to be, in a vague sort of way, apprehensive and uneasy.

"I was coming up later to see you about your typewriter," Nils said. "I thought I warned you to get rid of it."

In point of fact, he had warned me more than once, but my typewriter was almost new—a Swedish-made portable and a lovely little machine—and naturally enough I did not want to part company with it. I knew I would never get another. "I haven't been able to exchange it yet," I told him.

"Where is it now?"

"In my bedroom."

"I'll take it with me."

I nodded, and he took it away that night.

I was really very angry, but there was nothing I could do, and at heart I knew Nils would not have done this without a good reason. Months later I found out that by a freakish coincidence the stencils for the Resistance newssheet which circulated widely in Oslo were cut by an identical portable. They were not very common machines, and anyone searching my apartment could have connected my machine with the production of the illicit sheet and got me in serious trouble.

Pettersen came with me across the yard and at the entrance in the side street handed me my bag. I could tell by the way he watched me that he knew something was up. Perhaps what was in the bag did not feel to him like clothes I was going to exchange for food. But he said nothing.

9

LEONORA LOADS GOLD

I TRAVELED to Maritim without exciting any interest, but when I was within sight of the basin my nerve began to fail. How was Jan going to get past the *statspoliti?* How was I going to get past the sentry? At this point it would not have taken much to make me turn back, but nothing came along, so I just walked ahead until I came to the sentry box by the gap in the wire.

Here I stopped. The harbor was in darkness. I could only tell I had arrived at the gap because the box loomed up close and I could make out a reflection of starlight on the water. Not a thing was moving anywhere so far as I could see and I began to panic. Suppose something had gone wrong? Suppose Jan was not going to turn up? Suppose someone suddenly came out of the dark and asked me what I was doing there with a bag . . . ?

I listened for the tread of the sentries on the round I had earlier noted, out toward the breakwater and back. But there was not even the sound of slapping wavelets that one usually hears beside any large body of water. I was convinced that something was definitely wrong here, and very conscious that I was standing right against a sentry box from which at any moment a guard might emerge to find me.

At that moment a man *did* come out of the box. He came out and turned quickly toward me, then I saw by his expression that he was *expecting* me. He took my bag and turned back toward the wire. I followed with my heart pounding against my ribs, and as we passed I saw there was no guard in the box. The dinghy was at the steps, with another man on it. I had seen neither before, but from the description Jan had given me I knew that the man in the boat was the Norwegian, Birger. He looked like a sailor who had served his time on the lower deck.

We pulled in silence away from the quay, turning in and out of the moorings. I could not see six feet in front of me but Birger seemed to have little difficulty in making the *Leonora*. Strong hands pulled me aboard, and the dinghy was shipped without delay. She was housed on the decking over the cabin, lashed upside down. In the screened light of the cabin I recognized Jan. He seemed very glad to see me, and for my part I now felt that everything was all right.

"Did you come with anyone?" he asked me.

I shook my head, surprised. "You look all in, Jan."

"I've just spent an hour with these two carrying the boxes aboard. It is not easy work, I can tell you. Anyone see you come?"

"I never saw a soul."

"Not even your drunken Dutchman with the mustache?"

"It was very dark."

"Well, I saw the chap you mean this afternoon. He was still hanging around the café. I'd like to know what a man like that would be doing around here."

"This fly-by-night business has affected your mind," I told him.

"Well—the worst of it's over, and all should be plain sailing now. If he's up to no good he must still be guessing."

"When do we start?"

"Any moment now."

"Won't they try to stop us?"

Jan was dressed in a heavy sweater, an old pair of pants, and rope-soled shoes. He had a knitted cap and looked far from his usual neat self. But in a strange way I liked him better like this. He looked more like a man of action; a man who knew his way around among other men of action. He looked at home, grimy and disheveled. He was also far less polite to me.

"Nothing has moved out of this place for months. It's a morgue. No one is expecting anything to move out."

"What about the police on the quayside?"

"Did you see any police there? They've been taken care of, and you haven't seen these engines yet! You may not even feel them. She's a lovely boat. You should hear Birger on the subject."

At that moment I heard the grinding sound of starters engaged. It stopped; I felt the faint tremor of engines turning over. As Jan said, they made no sound, but of course with a modern cabin cruiser there is nothing unusual in that. I pulled myself up the companion and stood with my shoulders at deck level watching the moored craft slide by.

Jan had moved forward with the other two men and I had the night to myself.

Whoever was taking the *Leonora* out knew this harbor. It turned out to be Birger, but it could easily have been Jan's personal henchman, the Dutchman Erik, who also knew the waters intimately. No one attempted to stop us. In a short time the *Leonora* was clear of the huddle and headed out to the angle of the breakwater. The tower light —now not working, of course—showed its shape faintly silhouetted against an overcast sky. The swell made itself felt under my feet as the *Leonora* lifted and dipped. Almost before I realized, the boat had slipped through and was headed out into the open fjord.

No lights showed, but German warships were hardly a mile away to port now. No coastal shipping would be moving and the control was said to be strict. Harbor launches and German small craft would be patrolling, some of them with powerful searchlights. We would have trouble from these unless we were lucky. I could see where Oslo lay behind us from the slightly blacker outlines of the hills against the sky. My heart had stopped panicking and I felt very much happier now. I went forward and asked the men if they would like me to make coffee.

In the galley was a triple-burner primus cooker which ran on kerosene under pressure and produced a very hot flame. I was surprised to find a large quantity of real coffee and a quantity of butter and sugar—more than I had seen together in one place since the Germans came. I made the coffee—it smelled delicious—and carried it forward, balancing against the swell. Not much of a sea was running and the air of the fjords smelled very good.

I stayed with the men to enjoy my scalding coffee. A faint blue light was thrown over the instruments, including the compass, and in this light Birger's face showed, a sailor's face, clear of all expression, blank of thought. He was steering a course and letting the rest of the world go by. Jan was smoking a cigar at the helmsman's side. Erik sat on a shelf that could be made into a bunk, staring out into the darkness. I shall long remember that scene, for suddenly all the inside of the cabin jumped into a blinding relief as if a magnesium flare had been lit amongst us. I heard Birger swear, and the next thing I knew the boat was keeling over under full throttle to starboard and the blinding light was gone.

"Get aft," Jan ordered, and I left, but I could still see them peering into the darkness at the long finger of the searchlight that had picked us up. I stood as before with my shoulders on deck level, watching the night with the others, waiting for something to happen—and it came. The finger swept in a small arc over the sea and came on the *Leonora* again. Birger threw the boat about, changing course and zigzagging, throwing up a bow wave as she approached her maximum speed, but this time the light stayed with us and I knew that trouble lay ahead. Boats using the harbor had to be back at their moorings by nightfall. If found in the fjord they were escorted back and the crew arrested. The boat was seized. This was a standing German order, so we knew what we had to do.

We were by now out in the open fjord, which at this point is some five or six miles across from shore to shore. The open sea is roughly forty miles to the south and the waters are well sheltered by the hills; navigation holds no special dangers for anyone who knows the fjord. Birger left his throttle controls open and let the *Leonora* feel full power. For some time I kept aft as ordered, but in the end my curiosity took me back to the cockpit. Although we were driving ahead, the light was still on us, no closer it seemed, yet still there.

"Whoever's chasing us has a fast boat and he's holding on," Jan told me. "It's just a patrol boat. I'm not worrying."

"Maybe she's much farther back than you think," Birger said. "It's hard to tell in the dark. She may be pulling up on us. But she's using as much fuel as we are. Let's keep moving until we get down the fjord here a little and through the Droebaksund. I'll lose the joker then!"

The men had evidently been discussing tactics and were not agreed. Jan's face was drawn; he had a tense, concentrated look that bore out what he had said about the lust for gold. He looked like a man who was not going to stop at anything—and so did Birger. This did not quite fit into the peaceful expedition I had imagined.

The fjord narrows opposite the fortress of Oscarsborg—which I knew must be somewhere hereabouts—and I could just make out now, as we forged ahead, that we must have entered the Droebaksund. Here in daylight it is possible to see from bank to bank, and I realized that we could not hope to escape our pursuers until we reached open water again. It was lucky the *Leonora* was so speedy.

Beside the helmsman's stool was a carbine ready to hand, and I had a notion that there had been other arms about the cockpit which someone had hidden away when they heard me coming.

"Who do you think can be chasing us?" I asked Jan.

"If it's not a German patrol boat someone must have tipped someone off. A German naval craft would have had our legs. This chap hasn't. We're losing him—if we can last long enough. Going through the Droebaksund is like going through a tunnel."

"How much fuel have we?"

"Enough to take us out to sea and bring us back again, even at this rate, but of course getting out to sea is the last thing I want to do. Round here there's shelter and we'll get by, but out at sea we should be picked up for certain."

He looked at me for a moment, then beckoned me quietly out. In the cabin amidships he lowered himself onto a bunk.

"Look, Helen," he said. "I'm sorry about this, but I'm not going to let any Quisling gangsters hijack my gold. I had no idea anything like this would happen when I asked you if I could use your farmhouse. I suppose I ought to explain now that what we have aboard is—well, considerable. Come and look!"

Farther aft, over the engines, were large lockers, and in the light of a torch Jan showed me three cases made of heavy timber. They were not large cases, not much bigger than an average suitcase, yet Jan told me each case was all that the three men could lift. The wood had stencil marks on it and also seals in red wax which had been broken. There was no doubt that we had a "considerable" sum of money aboard.

"There are several of us in this," he said. "I have banker friends in occupied Holland who put me up to it. Quite a lot of capital belonging to quite a few worthy citizens in these uncertain times is tied up here in this boat."

"If there are a lot of people in this, the secret will leak out, as secrets always do."

"Maybe. There's always that risk. But no one except Erik knew where I was moving the stuff—or *when*. I can't understand who's after us."

"Birger?" I queried.

"He knows nothing. Just a paid hand. In it for the fun of the thing. I can vouch for him. He's well paid."

"This looks like the bullion banks hold in their vaults," I said.

"That's what it is. Gold money. Gold bars. It's been under cover for some time. Lots of people have been trying to save their capital—get it out of Europe to the Americas. And others have been following the trail trying to get it."

"Isn't it dangerous?"

"Possibly, if too much becomes known. That's why we wanted to tuck the gold away somewhere no one could know, and leave it for a while. Cross the trail."

I was a little ruffled to think there was more in this trip than I had been told, for I considered that if my house was to be used as a hiding place, at least Jan should have been completely frank. But when I came to turn what he had told me over in my mind, I realized that Jan would perhaps not have considered himself free to talk since the interests of others were involved. And he had told me as soon as we were at sea, after all. I felt less anxious.

At that moment Erik came back and announced, "Birger says the islands should be ahead."

10

LYING UP

THE NIGHT was dark except in our immediate neigborhood and I could see nothing, but Birger knew where he was by the darker shapes against the sky line. "The tide is just about right. I can take you right in."

Jan nodded. "So long as you know where you are."

It was impossible to see anything at all of our pursuers except a dazzling pinpoint of light a long way off. The light itself lay on us steady as a rock, as if it had been glued there, leaving us marooned in the darkness in a patch of light. It would have been easy enough, Jan told me, to dodge out of the beam for a while, but we would be picked up again in open water. The *Leonora* was white and conspicuous.

When Birger gave the word, Jan took the wheel and I watched Erik and Birger prepare something on deck. They poured a heap of gray powder on an old frying pan from the galley and added, I think, a handful of salt. Then Birger sent Erik to the cockpit to relay his signal. *"Alt klart?"* Erik asked. I heard Jan's reply *"Ja."*

A blinding flash hammered the darkness. The *Leonora*

95

turned immediately in her own length, flinging me heavily against the companion, and when I had recovered my balance I saw that all around us the sea was dimly lit by reflection. But we were streaking out of it. At first, I could not see why this should be. The *Leonora* was pulling out of the area at terrific speed, her bow waves showing in the half-light, and I then noticed what had escaped me before. The searchlight was on a drifting cloud of white smoke from the powder Birger had touched off. It no longer held the *Leonora*.

"Let that smoke last for another minute and we're O.K.," Birger said. "It will melt and leave them with nothing in their sights. They won't know where they are. And we're in among the islands now. . . ."

He strolled back, wiping his hands on a rag, to take over the wheel, and soon slacked off the engines to a tick-over cruising speed among the rocks I could now make out quite near at hand. We cruised on for some time and the atmosphere in the cockpit was very different. Until then I had not fully realized the strain the men had been under.

"What's your plan now?" Jan asked.

Birger seemed to have become the man in charge. "If this is the place I think it is," he said, "I know a landing that's used by the fishermen in really bad weather. There's a *hytte* on the island and the land is well-protected. Only an airplane would spot the *Leonora*—and not even then if you wanted to go to the trouble of covering her with branches. My advice would be for you to lie up during daylight. I don't like this business. Those jokers seemed to know too much for a German boat. They were never near enough to identify us for sure, yet they hung on. Why?"

"I'd like to know," Jan said. "Find your place and we'll lie up." He turned to me. "I'm sorry, Helen. We should have been almost at your place by now. But we'll make it in the dark tomorrow. Better safe than sorry."

It seemed to become lighter inshore; soon Birger picked up a bearing. He took us into a channel that formed a natural harbor and we made fast by flashlight. Then Birger led us over the rocks to the ruins of a *hytte* among the pines. The shutters were hanging, some of the timbers were agape, but the roof evidently was still weatherproof and the kitchen snug and warm. I helped Birger cook a meal on the stove with provisions carried from the *Leonora,* and that night all of us, except Birger who remained aboard the boat, slept at the *hytte.* Jan made up a bed for me between the stove and the wall where I slept very comfortably.

When light came next day I went out to look at our mooring. Jan warned me not to show myself on the open side of the island, so I kept to the channel. The mountains and pines came steeply down to the fjord here, and our little island lay not far from the mainland. The *Leonora* was tucked away in the shadow of the hillside; in her white paint she looked very conspicuous to me. Birger gave me a wave from the cockpit, and I invited him up to the *hytte* to eat. As far as I could see, there was not another human habitation or another ship in sight. The island itself blocked off most of the view of the fjord outside. There did not seem to be even a roadway through the pine forest.

Birger came ashore with a leap and I saw he had the carbine over his shoulder. He was a pleasant sort of man with a rather cheeky grin, but there was a cold, blue look in his eyes that warned you he would make an implacable enemy. I decided he was a good man for Jan to have brought along on this gold-running cruise. You got the impression he had seen a few similar jaunts in his time and that he knew most of the tricks of the trade. I wondered if he was with the Resistance but could not ask him, of course. It occurred to me then that Jan had expected trouble, and he had brought Birger along to take care of it.

"I mustn't leave the boat for long, Miss," he said. The "Miss" that seemed to be current on the *Leonora* was subtly flattering.

"She looks safe enough to me."

He shook his head as he helped me over the scattered boulders on the foreshore. "I'd like to get some pine branches over her decks. Aircraft."

I still wonder how much Birger knew. I am pretty sure he had been promised a fairly substantial reward for his help. He must have suspected something, if only from the weight of the cases. How he was to be paid and what the other arrangements were, I never knew. In Norway at that time no one pressed questions. Which I think about sums up the situation as far as Birger was concerned. I learned later that the cases had been delivered to the quayside and left there. Jan, with Birger and Erik to help, had manhandled them aboard one at a time in the dinghy. The crew couldn't have known where they had come from. Jan was a good strategist.

In a couple of minutes Birger had the kitchen organized and we cooked a big breakfast of bacon and eggs. There was plenty of butter and bacon, which with real coffee made a grateful meal. Shortly afterward Jan and Erik began to cut pine branches which they carried down to the *Leonora.*

Birger showed them how to camouflage the boat; in this art, too, he seemed to know his way around.

When they had finished this chore, Jan took me over the brow of the hill to look around our temporary hide-out. The east shore of the fjord was dotted with small islands. Some were a few hundred yards across, some only rocks. Nearby lay a larger island which in peacetime carried an unattended automatic navigational light. You could see the skeleton tower in the gray morning light.

"We might have used this place for our cache," Jan said. "We could have hidden the gold easily enough. But you never know. When we came to dig it up we might have found someone living on the top of it, and he might have objected."

"What are you going to do when we get to Cherry Trees?" Carsten had renamed the old farmhouse in English for my benefit; curiously enough, although it was lost in a wilderness of rocks and pine trees—to say nothing of common or garden nettles in the summer months—there were several flowering cherry trees of the sort that seem to bear no fruit.

"Leave the gold there and wait to see what happens—I mean with the European situation. Governments come and go, you know. The lucky citizens were the really wealthy ones; they got their money across the Atlantic before anyone thought of stopping them." Then he paused. "I thought you might have married me. I let my hopes run away with my planning."

"I'm sorry, Jan."

"It cannot be helped. Although I still think you are being foolish. You cannot cling to a dream all your life."

"It isn't a dream. I was—very happy."

"You have a long time to live yet."

"I'm sorry, Jan. But that's the way it is."

He shook his head. He was in some ways a most sympathetic and understanding man, and I could more logically have understood anyone like me wanting to marry him rather than not. But the fact remains I did not want to, and if you do not follow your own secret heart you are risking too much.

From the top of the hill I could see the fjord stretching away to the horizon. The mountains seemed cold and remote, the water gray and cruel. A German destroyer was steaming out to sea abreast of the island, making speed, by the look of her bow wave, and there was shipping in the channel. A German air-sea rescue launch was streaking back toward the air base outside Oslo. It all seemed very peaceful and orderly, as shipping always does to me.

Then Jan laid a hand on my arm and quickly drew me under the shelter of a stone wall. A German seaplane— one of the machines moored to buoys in the harbor at Oslo —appeared over the cliff's edge. The rocks must have screened the sound of its engines because we saw it before hearing it. It was flying very low and slowly, for, like all those seaplanes, it was designed for easy landings and takeoffs in restricted spaces, and was not fast.

The seaplane headed over the island, turning twice off course, then circled over the larger island nearby and finally disappeared back to the south again. Jan seemed disturbed, although I thought that this might well be only a routine patrol. The whole coast line around the fjord was patrolled by German surface craft and by Luftwaffe sea-

planes, yet in spite of this many Resistance men got away
by sea in small boats to join the Norwegians in Britain.

We hurried back to the *hytte* and Jan went down to the
Leonora to consult with Birger. He was not aboard long.
The two men came scrambling back up the foreshore and
hurried past the *hytte,* waving us inside. From the hillside
that overlooked the roof they surveyed the scene below,
then rejoined us.

"No smoke," Birger said. "When I heard the plane I
thought we might have smoke showing. They must know
no one lives on the island. Lucky you were burning pinewood."

"Was that the Luftwaffe?" I asked.

"Birger says more likely the Norwegians—Quisling pi-
lots in the coastal service . . . who else?" Jan demanded.

Birger shrugged.

"Let the fire go out. Use the galley aboard for cooking,
or if you like I'll bring you the primus stove."

We ate our midday meal on the *Leonora.* Shortly be-
forehand we had a visit from another aircraft following
the coast. Evidently they did not spot the *Leonora,* but I
did not like the look of things. I was not frightened, for I
was too tied up in the safe tradition of believing that
though you may read about things happening to other
people these were not the sort of things that would happen
to you. I only wished that we were safe at Cherry Trees.

When at length it was dusk we immediately set sail. Jan
and Birger carefully cleared up traces of our visit as far as
was possible at the *hytte.* We buried the empty cans, leaving the pine branches cut as camouflage on the foreshore
for the tide to carry away.

"How far are we from Larkollen?" I asked Birger. We were edging round the south corner of the island into the channels that led out into the fjord—a dangerous business in the gathering darkness, but it did not seem to trouble the Norwegian.

"I should say about forty minutes."

"You have to cross the shipping lane?"

"There's nothing about after nightfall. No landmarks or navigation lights, so the shipping lies up."

"No navigation lights on the ships, either, to show us where they are."

"Nothing will run us down. I only hope we do see no lights!"

After we had safely headed into the last channel before open water, I left the cockpit and went aft. Jan was in the cabin. He was cleaning a Walther pistol and when he had finished and loaded the long magazine he tucked rounds away in his pockets, together with a spare magazine. "I'm going to be ready," he said. He got up to pour me a drink, and when we had the glasses he gave me a toast.

"Here's to gold!"

"To Cherry Trees," I substituted. I distrusted this cargo now, and I suddenly had a yearning for the old familiar place.

11

CHERRY TREES FARM

THE FARM at Larkollen had once belonged to my husband's maternal grandmother. She was born there, and I always understood that in those times the land was intensively farmed. The title deeds went back to the seventeen hundreds, but for years the place had been used only as a summer retreat. I had been ideally happy there with Carsten and Kirsti when she was a baby. The land itself had long since gone back to a mountainside wilderness; the only relics of cultivation you would notice were the orchard trees and the nettles. In Norway, nettles seem to follow cultivation. Along the fjords old farmhouses are generally invested with Norwegian nettles, guaranteed to discourage bare legs and sea bathing. At the moment I yearned to get there, away from the war; away from all this hide-and-seek.

I soon felt by the motion that we were out in the fjord. Some time passed while I talked idly with Jan in the cabin. I remember thinking we must be over the dangerous shipping lane, and maybe halfway to dear old Cherry Trees and its nettles, when suddenly the light was on us once more.

It lit the deck outside the darkened cabin and Jan leaped to his feet to get to the cockpit. There was no doubt about it; the chase was on again.

Alone in the cabin amidships I felt a tremor as the engines throbbed to their full power. And then a queer thing happened to me. My whole world shrank around me. The close white walls, the blackened portholes, the bunks with their sponge-rubber mattresses—all this seemed to come to a sharper, more intimate focus.

It was in this moment of awareness that I saw the situation clearly for the first time. I thought: What a fool I've been to get mixed up in something like this. I should have confided in someone before committing myself to this dangerous business. I should have told Nils. I should never have started out. If the Germans were after us they would get us in the end. You could never shake the Germans off. They were a race who kept on and on until they got what they wanted. I was afraid. Afraid of something vague but in itself real, for some instinct told me that, whatever it was, it was going to happen to me. I had a hopeless feeling that we would never be rid of the searchlight, that wherever we moved it would follow.

What would happen to Kirsti if I disappeared and the Germans could not trace me? The first thing they would do would be to take her away and hold her as a hostage.

How long I stood there thinking in this way I do not know. There was no sound in the boat now except the faint hum of the engines. There was hardly any motion to show our speed. But all the time on the roof of the cabin, which was the underside of the decking above, there was this curtain of light from the searchlight behind us—the light that followed us like a ghost.

What right had I, a mother with a small child, to be in a mess like this? I was asking now. There was no answer, of course, but with it came a dull sort of anger—directed against Jan.

In the end I went forward to the men. My mind was made up. I had had enough of this and I was not going to cooperate any further. They could do what they wished. I was getting out at the first opportunity. In theory, all very well. But how was I going to carry it out? For the moment I kept my own counsel.

I found out from Birger that by bad luck whatever craft was out patrolling, looking for us, anticipating our making a dash to get away from the area, had begun to sweep with her searchlight just as we were well out in the open. She picked the *Leonora* up with the first sweep, and this time she began the chase closer to us.

"Don't worry," Birger said. "We'll make it. We'll out-run them again. Only risk is an engine failure, and with these Scottish jobs we're on velvet. They've got more to worry about than we have. There are plenty more islands over the other side, Miss. Cheer up!"

I noticed then that the whole armory was out in the open. The carbine was back in the corner and Jan's Walther was on the bunk alongside other weapons ready for action. "I think you'd better get aft," Jan said, but I told him coldly that I intended to stay and see what happened.

"All right, as you wish. But if they fire you must lie down on the cabin floor."

I do not remember much about the rest of our run. My mind was occupied with thoughts of what I must do. The craft that was chasing us seemed a long way away to me and we obviously held our lead. No one opened fire on us. In fact, the night was curiously black and still. It was only half-real—like a dream. We seemed to have the water to ourselves. In any event, the chase did not last long, for a curious piece of luck came our way.

We must have been on a course that unwittingly took us close astern of an unseen tramp steamer making up toward Oslo, for suddenly the light that held us went out like a snuffed candle. One moment the *Leonora* was hazily outlined in a mantle of dim white; the next, darkness swallowed us up. The searchlight had been cut off by this tramp, which now could be seen with a kind of soft fan, a halo behind her silhouetting her outline and touching her rigging and her bridge with a tenuous tracing of light like frost on early-morning cobwebs. In a way it was very beautiful, but Birger wasted no time on aesthetics. He swung the *Leonora* to a new course that kept her in this patch of shadow, screened by the steamer, and in a short time we were able to get in among the islands. The light did not pick us up again.

After a while I went back to the cabin. I heard the engines slack off; then the door opened and Jan came in. From the first I thought he looked very strange. He did not look like the man I had known.

"That's got rid of them," he said. "The swine."

"Why did you risk bringing the *Leonora*—and them— so close to Larkollen?" I asked.

He looked up sharply from tapping a cigarette on the back of his case. "No risk. There's nothing to connect us with your place—yet. We've lost them in the islands, anyway, and what would be more natural than to run for cover here?"

"Jan," I said. "I don't want whoever is chasing you anywhere near Cherry Trees. I don't want them near Larkollen. I didn't bargain for this."

"We're headed for Larkollen. You seem to have forgotten that."

The way he held my eyes was domineering. It had an
arrogance that curiously enough helped me to go through
with what I had to say.

"I had not forgotten it. I simply do not want this boat
or your gold anywhere near my house."

His face changed then. It seemed to twist, under pressure from his sudden rage. "I don't think I quite understand you."

"I don't want your cases of gold at Cherry Trees."

I saw a vein in his neck throb and his lips tightened to
a thin slit. "I cannot change my plans at a moment's notice
on a woman's whim."

"This is no whim."

"We are going to Cherry Trees."

"No. I'm not going to have your cases there!"

He laughed—it was a nasty sound—then he moved
closer to me. "Just as a matter of interest, I'd like to know
how you can stop me?"

I tried to hold his eyes, but they looked so different. In
this moment of frustration his whole nature seemed to have
changed. "If you persist I shall go to the police and tell
them what's hidden there."

"You'll have to explain how it got there. But—you're
not really serious?"

"I'm just letting you know I don't want to be mixed up
in it."

He must have been under a great strain, for he lost patience and took my wrist, forcing me back into a chair. "You're in, and you're staying in!" he shouted. "How can I change my plans now?"

"You're hurting me!"

He let go of my arm at once. "You think I could turn back now and give up just because you're panicking? You're a woman and under strain. By tomorrow you'll be laughing at the state you got into. Helen—please be advised by me. Be reasonable!"

He backed away toward the door, still very angry. "Understand, I'm not fooling now!"

"I think you don't know what you're doing! I think you are out of your mind," I said.

"Well, go on thinking that, my dear, but stay here in the cabin like a good girl."

I heard the key turn in the lock.

As it turned out, I did not have very long to reflect, for soon the purr of the engines slacked away again and I heard the small waves slap at the *Leonora*'s hull. For a while we lay rocking gently in the swell, then the engines started up anew and we were going astern. I was tempted to unscrew the porthole and look out but I did not want to attract attention, possibly a hail of bullets from our pursuer —if he was still pursuing. I felt the craft swing, then forge ahead for a while, then the engines gave a short bump and I heard the sound of someone taking up a mooring. Then all was quiet. It appeared we had arrived at wherever it was Jan had decided we were going to hide out the rest of the night.

An age passed, then a key sounded in the lock and Birger entered. He had a tray with food and a mug of steaming coffee. "Where are we?" I asked him.

"Larkollen." He put down the tray. "I could have done with you in the galley," he said. "We got rid of those jokers O.K. and now here we are—safe enough from the look of things. What did you do to His Lordship? He's blown his top and is biting everyone's head off."

I decided I could do no harm by talking a little to Birger.

"Near these moorings is a house that belongs to me. It's the only house for miles and I don't want this craft anywhere near my jetty. I don't want a gun battle around my house. I don't want it burned down. If the Germans are after us, they'll burn it down, and we'll all get shot."

"Well, it isn't the Germans."

"Why not?"

"If that had been a patrol boat she would have called out others. We should have had a hornet's nest of craft after us—all faster than we are."

"Then who is it?"

"I'd certainly like to know."

"What about the seaplane?"

"Might have been looking for us. Might not. Someone may have put it onto us. A private person. Some tough character from the place where he used to keep those cases." He moved a dish and looked up at me sharply. I think he was as puzzled as I was, but he had a theory. "Somebody found out something is going on and wants to get a slice for himself. There's plenty of that sort around these days. Anyway, don't fret yourself about it being the—Germans,

Miss. This is a private fight—take it from me! Count the
Heinies out."

"Including a German pilot from the seaplane base?"

"Maybe the Luftwaffe pilot was doing him a favor—
for a consideration. But I can see you wouldn't want any of
them at your house, Miss. I've got to lock the door again."

"Where are we tied up?"

"We've picked up a buoy in mid-channel. But I
shouldn't try anything. You couldn't make it. Besides, we're
moving before first light." He came back from the door to
lower his voice. "He's got the oars from the dinghy by his
bunk forward. Seems His Lordship doesn't trust anyone.
Good night, Miss."

"Good night, Birger," I said.

I ate the meal he had provided, but with little appetite.
I was too upset. At that now familiar table between the
bunks, I drank my coffee and smoked a cigarette. I had
plenty to occupy my thoughts but for a long while nothing
seemed real. I could not bring myself to believe in things
as they were. It was too fantastic. The difficulty was in ac-
cepting Jan Goffinger as a man harsh, arrogant, overbear-
ing, with his mind ruthlessly applied to one end—the
precious hoard of gold he had managed to save out of the
chaos of Hitler's Europe!

Men will do anything for gold, he had told me. He
should have added, "And that includes me." I did not know
what to expect next. After all, I had said I would tell the
police, and it would only be common sense in a man who
worked things out as carefully as Jan to see that I did not
get the chance. With this disturbing thought I settled down
to wait.

12

LEONORA'S VISITOR

THE BOAT seemed very quiet. There was not a
sound in the night outside apart from the faint slap slap of
the wavelets against our hull—one of the most peaceful
sounds in the world, just as the gentle weaving of the reflection of sunlight from those same wavelets on the roof
of a small boat cabin is to my mind the most restful sight
in the world. Jan would have gone ashore in the dinghy, no
doubt—although I had not heard him. Perhaps even at this
very moment he was at Cherry Trees?

The thought angered me afresh and I rolled myself
from the bunk. Jan Goffinger was a brave man, but also ex-
tremely pigheaded. Once he had made his plans he liked to
carry them through. Then I realized the gold was still
aboard, otherwise I would surely have heard them dragging those cases. He must be out prospecting, I decided.

I determined to see what I could see, and attempted to
unscrew the porthole. This, like most butterfly nuts, needed
a tap to start it, and I used what a woman would use in the
circumstances— the heel of a shoe. The nut gave and I un-

111

screwed it. I switched off the cabin light, and after an interval to give my eyes time to get used to the darkness, I opened the scuttle. The familiar smell of pines and of creosote and of salt seemed to stretch out to greet me—a nostalgic and heady perfume. I could make out the vague shape of landmarks in the darkness, and after a while I distinguished the hump of rock where our steps led down to the sandy beach. I could not make out the gable of the house. This was Larkollen, sure enough. But there was no sign of life.

The door opened behind me. As I jumped back from the porthole I saw the circle of a flashlight on the floor and a voice said, "Shut that porthole!"

I shut it and waited for the circle of light to come up. It flicked over the porthole, then slid along to the switch on the bulkhead. A hand moved into the circle and the cabin lights came on. I saw the intruder was Erik.

"Trying to get out?" he asked.

"I was looking out . . . at familiar things," I answered. The Dutchman looked anything but well-disposed toward me.

"Or trying to let someone in?"

"I was just looking out at my house in the dark."

"Well, let me tell you this. The Boss has left me here aboard for the night to keep an eye on you, and he's told me what to do if you start any nonsense such as trying to escape or making signals—see? You'll keep the ship darkened and leave the portholes be. And stay where you are. You've messed us up enough as it is. I'm not squeamish about women, see?"

"How could I signal?" I asked him. "This is the only

house for miles. The nearest neighbor is on Tinnholmen,
the island out in the fjord there, and he's a Quisling."

"Never mind who it belongs to. Don't let me hear you
knocking the portholes open again."

"You won't."

He pushed the automatic pistol he was holding in his
right hand into its holster, closed the door behind him, and
turned the key.

Not a soul knew I was here. All over Norway people
were being killed night and day—would one more make
much difference, if one of them tonight happened to be
me? How long I sat on the bunk alone with my fears, I do
not know, but at length the sound of the dinghy returning
made itself evident. I heard soft steps on the deck and felt
the boat itself shift—in a craft of this size you can feel even
one person moving, especially abeam. I had taken my boots
off and was sitting hunched, knees to chin, in my slacks
and a sweater. I rose now and listened at the door. A sound
of men's voices came to me from forward, then steps
sounded overhead. They were evidently getting back into
the dinghy. I risked unscrewing the porthole again. With
Birger about I felt less afraid of Erik.

I saw the dinghy with two shadowy figures aboard making for the jetty. Someone overhead was shifting his feet
as he waited. Then the dinghy came back with one person
in her and the man overhead got in. Once more the small
craft made the jetty and this time it did not come back. I
was alone in the *Leonora*. The luminous face of the clock
told me it was nearly four o'clock in the morning.

If I could break down the door, I could get out of the
cabin, but that would not help much unless I was ready to

swim ashore in freezing cold sea water. I wondered if Jan
had now found somewhere to hide away his treasure.

In the end I decided there was nothing I could do to
help myself out of the situation at the moment, so I shut the
porthole, switched on the light, and tried to read a book.

Much later I heard someone moving again.

The dinghy was being made fast over my head, but
there seemed something furtive about the movements.
Had someone come back to fetch me? I was the only outside
person who knew about the gold—and so they had to come
to terms with me. Or—

I heard a stealthy footfall on the deck. It went forward,
then for some time silence fell again over the *Leonora*. In
the locker was a heavy flashlight which I groped for and
found. If I could hit anyone with that it might stop him for
a while. Meanwhile I could only wait.

Steps sounded outside the forward door of the cabin. I
heard the knob turn—one way, then the other. Each time I
also heard the panels creak as a shoulder was pressed
against them. I thought wildly: The lock has stuck or perhaps he has forgotten the door is locked. *Perhaps it's someone who doesn't know it's locked!*

I shall never forget the next few minutes. They seemed
to stretch on and on, and all the time I knew I was on the
edge of a scream. It was the unknown element that scared
me. I did not know who this was. Anything might happen
to me in the next few minutes and there was nothing I
could do to stave it off. Inaction and uncertainty are the
prime factors in panic; I realize that well enough now.

The door creaked and strained; then I began to dis-
tingush a new sound. Someone was levering the lock away

from the bulkhead. I heard the sharp cracking of splintering wood. For a moment I thought Birger might be getting in to help me, but then I realized that he would at least have called out to reassure me.

At some point my panic reached its height and began to recede. Common sense came back to me to some limited extent. I realized that this man at the door could not know anyone was in the cabin. It was not Birger, who would have whispered to me. It could not be Jan or Erik. Might it not be some local lad, out for loot in these troubled times? Here was a luxury craft left unattended, probably illegally at these moorings. . . . It might even be a Resistance man having a look around at an unexpected craft in his area. I began to take courage. The lock had splintered by now, and at any moment my visitor might come in. I called out boldly, "Who's there?"

The effect was electrical. I heard something fall to the boards, then a scuffle of feet. Next moment there was a splash. When I reached the door my flashlight showed it open and I was soon on deck. Now that action had come I found I was no longer afraid. I risked flashing the beam over the water.

A man was swimming strongly only a few yards away from the side of the *Leonora,* heading for the jetty which was about thirty yards off. He cast a scared look at the boat and redoubled his efforts. In that moment I saw his face quite clearly. It was the man I had seen at Maritim—the drunken sailor outside the café who had followed me with his bleary eyes the afternoon I conned the *Leonora* for Jan.

13

A GAME OF HIDE-
AND-SEEK

I WAS too astonished to move. This sailor's appearance at Larkollen was so unexpected. I could think of no reason why he should be prowling around the boat, apparently looking for something, unless he knew someone was moving a quantity of gold. He evidently must have been watching the *Leonora,* since he expected her to be unmanned. That meant he must have been lying in wait for the *Leonora* and keeping her under observation.

I had switched off the flashlight, but I could still hear him swimming in the stillness of the night. Soon he was clawing at the wooden supports of the jetty. I could have caught him in the beam again, but I let him go. From the sound of his steps on the wooden planking he still seemed to be in a considerable hurry. The noise ceased as he reached the sand.

I came to life again. I knew that dawn would soon be showing over the hills and that Jan and Erik might be back at any moment. Nothing was going to keep me on this boat now. I flashed the light toward where I had heard the

116

sailor tying up and found our own dinghy, which served to confirm that he must have been keeping watch and have seen the three men go ashore. I collected my few belongings from the cabin and lowered myself into the dinghy, cast off, and rowed myself ashore. My relief at being away from the *Leonora* made me almost lightheaded. I felt that once I was inside my own house I would be safe and that I could start again—an illogical attitude but a very comforting one. I simply could not wait to get inside Cherry Trees.

I was fumbling in my haste to get inside and lock the door. The front door and the kitchen door at the old house were of very heavy timber and each had a steel bar the width of the door, which pivoted to fit into a steel slot in the wall. This kind of fastening is not uncommon in Norway, where sections are isolated for long periods each year, and it is no exaggeration to say that it would be far easier to cut through the wall of the house than through the door. The thought of those bars was like a magnet drawing me to the house. I couldn't move fast enough.

I tied the dinghy up to the jetty and half ran over the planking, jumping down to the sandy beach and across the lawn to make my way round to the back of the house. I showed a light in the woodshed and picked up the key from the place where we always kept it, then let myself in by the back door. The house smelled shut up, enclosed, unaired, unused. It smelled as it always did when we arrived to re-open it, and my heart warmed toward it. I knew no one had been inside the house, which gave me a sense of security again, false or not. I walked from room to room downstairs, flashing the light. The windows were all shuttered; everything was just as we had left it seven months before. I lit the oil lamp in the kitchen and placed it on the table.

My first thought was to start the stove and get some warmth in the place, but for the wood I would have to go outside again, and at this I checked. I had the senseless idea that if once I went outside Cherry Trees I would never get in again. And there was the dinghy, too. Should I not have dragged her up over the beach and hidden her away?

I opened the back door and looked out. It was beginning to get light. The dawn had stolen up on me.

Daylight gave me confidence. I stepped out into the yard and looked out over the fjord. The early light showed everything in sharp contrast as if it were a scene newly etched. The wooden piers of the jetty, the rocks, the sprawling shape of an old beachwall like a broken comb on the flat sand, the gulls starting their day's quest on the turn of the tide—all this seemed something caught half-awake by the new day. Something still halfway in dreamland. But the tangy early-morning smell was there as real as ever. The cold smell of the pines and the mountains and the salt is something you can never forget on the fjords. The troubles of civilization, the crowded towns and smoky hovels, the factories, the dead-eyed human beings tied to their desks and their account books and the police courts and sickbed hospitals—the smell of the fjords makes you forget all these things.

I walked down to the jetty and pulled the dinghy along to the sand and dragged her up to our boathouse. A long veranda runs above the beach at Cherry Trees. To the east is the boathouse, on a lower level, for the house is built on a promontory above the rocks which hang over the beach. A flight of steps cut in the rock leads up to the lawn from the shore, and abuts on the end of our jetty. The farm buildings lie behind the house, and a long garden goes back into the pine trees.

Back safe in the house, I realized that anyone would see the marks where the little dinghy had been dragged over the sand. Hauling the dinghy up was as good as saying publicly that if wanted I was to be found in the house. Had I left her tied to the jetty it would have been anyone's guess who had used her. But I could not have cared less. I brought in a huge pile of wood and started my stove, then in a state of siege I opened up cans and cooked myself a meal. I found I was quite hungry.

From time to time that morning I went upstairs to peer through the shutters at the *Leonora,* but nothing was moving. No one came out to her. No one visited the house. The day turned out to be sunny, with a hint of spring in the air. The snow had gone by now, but patches of it could be seen in the hills nearby. I knew I stood a good chance of being able to get through to the village.

To get to Viknaar normally took about an hour's walking—in Norway you measure by time, rather than by distance, as traveling is more up and down than roundabout, and the going varies considerably. The village was the nearest place for help. I was not going to the police. For one thing, I would have to explain how I was mixed up in the business—even I knew it was illegal to hoard gold. Probably it was even more illegal to try to move it. And, in truth, I did not want to get Jan into trouble. I just wanted help to get back to my daughter, and to forget about the whole ill-starred affair if that were possible.

I was reasonably sure I could get back to Oslo, but now I hesitated about leaving Cherry Trees. I had the queer feeling of not wishing to desert the house at a time like this. I had already seen what a change the lust for gold could bring about in a man like Jan, and I dreaded what they might do to the place. That is the only reason I can think of that made me decide to stay on. One can be brave in the light of a new and bracing day.

I busied myself about the house airing a bed and doing various jobs that kept me occupied. No one came near the boat all day, which struck me as very strange. I wondered if anything had happened to the three men. I could not know that they were busy digging until their hands were blistered on the little island of Rikeness about seven miles away to the southwest. Jan had found his new cache and Erik had broken into the farm buildings belonging to a nearby landowner—the wealthy Quisling I had mentioned to Erik in the cabin—to help himself to tools. Jan took a risk leaving the gold aboard the *Leonora* in the channel, but there was little else he could do in the circumstances.

Toward dusk I noticed a small boat in the distance. She appeared to be making away from the island toward the open fjord—possibly for the seaside resort of Moss farther up. Apart from that I saw nothing all day. When dusk fell and the gulls streaked with lazy beats of their wings against the sunset it became very quiet along the deserted strip of coast at Larkollen. From the inside of the empty house I could hear the faint *aah-aah* of the surf on the beach. The hissing crackle of the shingle swept by the tide was followed by a pause of utter silence until the distant, faintly sounding thud of the next breaker arrived to breathe, in an almost human way again, *Aah-aaaah!* Then the brittle, grating crackle of the shingle moving . . . and silence once more.

I can hear the sound of the surf at Larkollen at any time at will, waking or dreaming. It is one of the lovely sounds of my life and I shall never tire of it. But this night as the darkness gathered it had a remote, desolate sound and I began to wish I had not been so brave in daylight. I wished I had left for Viknaar.

"In the morning," I told myself. "First thing in the morning I shall leave. As soon as it is light I will go. . . ." I heaped the stove with wood and drew my chair close. Later I went over the house carefully, looking at every fastening, then I began to cook myself a supper out of the provision cupboard. I read a book over my meal, but all the time I had an ear strained to catch the sound of anyone prowling.

To be alone in a house produces a dreadful feeling of separation from one's fellow humans that grows as time passes. When you are alone in a house and danger threatens —or you imagine it threatens—the feeling is much worse. By the time it was bedtime I was ready to scream at nothing, and I imagined there was an intruder in every shadow. But in spite of my state of nerves, I never heard anyone drag the dinghy out from where I had hidden it—yet I learned later that early in the night the crew of the *Leonora* recovered their dinghy.

I had not slept for so long that I dropped off almost as soon as I tumbled into my improvised bed beside the stove.

How long I slept I do not know, but I remember distinctly waking at some time in the night and telling myself sleepily, "There's someone in the house." At the time I was not sure whether I was dreaming or actually awake but I drifted off again before I decided.

I was sleeping in the kitchen—a large room with a pinewood floor and a sloping roof dropping into the yard, which once upon a time was the farmyard. It was still pitch-dark when I awoke a second time to the definite sound of someone walking on the edge of the roof. I could hear the timbers creak, the faint scrape of boots on the shingles. What actually woke me was the noise of a broken shingle sliding down to fall into the yard. In a moment I was sitting up in bed with my heart hammering.

I could not delude myself. Someone was breaking into the house—and doing it in the obvious way. All was fast at ground level, so the visitor was trying the first-floor shutters. Instantly the picture in my mind was of Erik. "Jan has sent him to fetch me back!" I told myself. I knew then for certain that I had had enough of this affair. It is difficult to be brave in the middle of the night.

Soon I could tell by the sounds coming from above that the man had forced a shutter. With the intruder actually inside the house, I began to move. I realized that I could not pretend no one had been in the place. If he didn't already know I was there, the stove would betray me. You cannot hide a huge stove full of red-hot wood at a moment's notice. The only thing was to simulate flight. If a woman found herself trapped in a house by someone breaking in, what would her attitude be? I argued that she would run.

I left the kitchen just as it was and opened the back

1 Helen Astrop.

2 Sister Hjoerdis
   at Larkollen.

3 Kirsti.

4 The barn at Larkollen where Birger and Holter lay in wait.
Shown from the rear.

5 Helen Astrup in the door of a shed at Cherry Trees Farm where goat's-milk cheeses were usually stored.

6 The main house, Cherry Trees Farm.

7 Bridge near Oslo blown by Nils Berg's group. The negative of this photo was sent back by Shetland Bus to the British War Office.

8 Entrance to the National Teatret subway station in Oslo,
where Helen Astrup was to meet the British agent. On the day
this clandestine photograph was taken—February 17, 1942—
Resistance workers had marked many German signs with black
crosses such as the one circled here, in token of national mourn-
ing for executed Joessings.

9 Photograph taken by Nils Berg's group showing Germans searching the back of the Bogstadveien tobacco shop after Helen Astrup's escape. No member of the group was caught.

10 German soldier posting a notice—one of the many invaluable clandestine photos taken by the chemist's shopkeeper in Nils Berg's group. The risks of such photography are clearly evident here.

11 This photograph was taken from the window of a moving train and brought out of Norway by a British agent. It shows a group of prisoners on their way to camp. When the negative was examined in London, four of the men were identified: Nils Berg is second from the left.

12   Col. B. L. Jacot, who was dropped into Norway by parachute in 1942. The bridge in the photograph had been blown up by Resistance workers aided by British technicians, repaired by the Germans, and during the night following this early-morning scene was again blown, by the Resistance alone.

door. Then I made my way to the hall that reached from the front of the house to the back. Here, built into the huge central chimney stack—practically the only thing in the house not built of wood—was a brick-lined recess, originally some sort of bread-baking oven when that part of the house was the kitchen.

I opened the door of this tiny hole and squeezed in. Unless you knew the house intimately you would never have guessed the place even existed.

I curled up and lay silent in the oven. Soon I heard the man in the hall itself. A match grated. I imagined him looking around—looking straight at the oven. But he passed on and I breathed again.

Then an odd thing happened. In our dining room there is an old Norwegian court cupboard and this cupboard has a peculiarity. If you walk past it, the weight of your body on the age-old floor boards causes them to sag slightly, which has some effect on the cupboard. After you have gone by, one of the doors slowly begins to open. If you are new to the place you may notice it and turn to close it, but the cupboard door closes itself anyway as the floor boards rise again, so no one in the family bothers.

I found out something about the intruder, thanks to this cupboard. He must have groped his way past it without noticing the door. Then he must have turned back to retrace his steps, and in doing so caught his knee a crack on the slowly opening door. Anyway he let fly a string of oaths which showed he was Norwegian, a cultured Norwegian at that. I think that knowing this must have given me some sorely needed courage, for when I heard him go down the cellar steps—the cellars at Cherry Trees stretch the whole

width and length of the house and are very old—when I
heard him on the stone steps I climbed out of my oven and
crept along to have a peep at him.

The man had a flashlight which he shone before him
and the light, reflected from the stone, silhouetted his figure. I cannot say whether I knew it all along or whether I
was just incapable of further surprises, but I realized at
once that this was the same man who had broken the lock
on the cabin door of the *Leonora,* the same man who had
watched me at Maritim, and who I thought looked like a
Dutch sailor!

I stood at the top of the cellar steps listening to him
moving about below. He did not seem anxious to hide his
presence; perhaps he had seen the back door open and
imagined I had flown. When I heard him returning I ran
back down the hall. Outside the bread oven I hesitated. I
felt a sudden urge to be free, so I passed the cupboard and
ran up the stairs. I had the crazy idea then that I could slip
from room to room ahead of him. I stood on the landing
and listened to his movements in the kitchen. He was apparently helping himself to the remains of my canned
spaghetti and chopped ham. In the next half hour, while I
waited poised to fly at a moment's notice, he visited the
cellars twice.

After the second visit he turned down the hall and with
the light of his flashlight before him made for the stairs.
The light came very close to catching me on the banister
rail, but I ducked back just in time and ran noiselessly into
my room—a long room with a veranda over the channel.
To my horror, the steps came after me. For a moment I
thought they were going along the landing into another

room, but they creaked toward my door. I dived under the bed. Now I could see his shoes against the spotlight on the carpet.

I watched him go around the room, opening cupboards and looking in drawers. For a while he seemed interested in a pair of fur-lined boots, measuring them off against his huge palm. But he set them down in the end. It was then he turned his light on the bed. It came in sharply under the gathered hanging edge of the bedspread and lit up the underside of the springs by reflection. It seemed to me that the man was holding me in the beam, playing with me like a cat with a mouse. Suddenly the light swept on. At the door he turned back for a while to sweep the room again; then I heard his steps go from room to room, quietly and methodically. I don't think I could have moved to save my life.

Some time later I heard him in the kitchen again. By this time I had recovered my wits, so I crept out and listened again from the top of the stairs. My watch told me it was just after four o'clock in the morning, and I hoped he would leave before it began to get light. But he was taking his time. Finally I heard him reopening the back door. All was dark. I could see nothing. After a long time had elapsed without anything happening, I decided with a sigh of relief that my unwelcome visitor had gone.

I crept quietly down the stairs and tiptoed into the kitchen. It was empty but the back door was still open. I ran across the floor and shut and bolted it. Then I got the matches and removed the chimney of the lamp to light it. I had replaced the chimney when a voice spoke from just behind me, "Well, well! So the bird hasn't flown, after all?"

14

THE FLOWER SONG

I STOOD holding onto the back of a kitchen chair as if my life depended on the sureness of my grip. He was a huge man with a blond mustache and a lot of blond hair, muscular but with the slightly boiled, fishlike look that comes of some sort of glandular deficiency. His eyes protruded a little and his lip hung. I certainly do not like people with protruding eyes! The backs of his hands were covered with hair and he had tufts of wiry hair growing out of his ears.

He moved slowly and deliberately closer to me, but I could not have moved if the house had been on fire. My legs ceased to work for me. They had had enough and had packed up. What really frightened me was the realization that he had been behind the door, and that I had scraped by him when I went to bolt it, *thinking myself alone.*

"Well, aren't you going to say anything?"

I could only goggle at him, like a bird paralyzed by a snake. With his open hand he pushed me into a chair and

I sat down with a bump. "What are you doing in this house?"

Something began to tick over inside. If he was going to strangle me, sitting dumb wouldn't help. I might as well let him know that this was my house and that I was known in these outlandish parts.

"I'm here because it happens to be my house."

"So? And did you just happen to be on that boat?"

"I was on the boat."

"Thank you for the scare you gave me. You came ashore in the dinghy? And what did you do with it?"

"I dragged it up the beach."

"Did you see who took it?"

I shook my head. This was the first I had heard of its disappearance.

"You think they are back on the boat?"

"How do I know?"

"Why were you locked in the cabin?"

"I was trying to get away. To come here to my house for help. They wanted to stop me."

He took out a pack of cigarettes and lit one without taking his eyes off me. "I think you can help me," he said slowly. "I think you are going to help me against those men on the boat." This seemed to be a fairly common reaction produced on strong men by my type of helpless femininity.

"I'm not going to help anyone anywhere. You had no right to break into my house."

"In these days one does not always stop to ask permission. There is not always time to be polite in Norway in these days. I think you will tell me what you know about these men. Why have they left the boat?"

"I don't know anything about them. They are no friends of mine."

"Goerdler?"

"Who is he?"

He stared at me doubtfully. "What nationality are you? Dutch?"

"I'm English."

That seemed to surprise him. "What are you doing here in Norway?"

"I was married to a Norwegian. This was our home."

"So?" He dropped his eyes as he whittled away the ash of his cigarette. "Can I ask you to help me with those people out there? Will you let me stay in your house for a while when it gets light?"

"They will be sailing with first light," I told him.

"I want to watch them and make sure. They're up to no good. I have been watching them, you see."

"I know," I said.

"I must not lose them now. I just want to watch and make sure."

As long as I was free to leave as soon as it began to get light I did not mind what this man did. I had not been strangled yet, and felt more confident. But while I was de-bating what to reply, something happened that changed the whole situation.

My visitor was standing over me, his back to the inside door of the kitchen. I saw that door edge open. I watched pop-eyed as a figure slipped noiselessly into the room. The newcomer was outside the circle of light but I recognized him at once; it was the Norwegian, Birger, holding an automatic before him as he came. I scarcely had time to take this in before he said, "All right! Reach for it! And let's have no tricks."

The bigger man jumped around, saw the automatic pistol, and his hands sailed up over his head. Birger backed him against the wall and ran his hands over him. "Now sit at the table," he ordered, "and we'll have the lamp on the side here."

Birger carried the lamp to the kitchen dresser and stood there himself while he spoke to us. "What's *he* doing here?" he asked me.

"He broke in. He broke into the boat, too."

"Looking for something?" Birger asked him.

"Yes. You bet I'm looking for something. I'm not the only one."

"Oh, yes?"

"Use your head. We're looking for what you and Goerdler have got and we'll find it in the end."

"Who's Goerdler? And what's got into your heads, chasing us about the fjord with searchlights in these times? I suppose it was you?"

"Well, I can answer that one easily enough. As if you didn't know. Do you think you can play about with four million kroner worth of gold without attracting a certain amount of attention?"

"*Four million?* You're crazy!"

"That's what's aboard that boat, and you're not going to get away with it."

"You're trying to lift it?" Birger was watching the other closely.

"We're *going* to lift it!"

"Who are you, anyway?"

"That would be telling."

Birger turned to me; I could see now that he was grinning. "I wanted to see if you were here. I've quit over there
—as you might say. His Lordship's gone clean off his rocker.
He's got worse all along and he's just about raving now."

"How did *you* get away?" the other man asked.

"You mind your own affairs and I'll mind mine. How do
you think?"

"He'll come after you."

"He's leaving at first light, and no one knows I've gone
—so far. He won't stop to chase around after me; I'm only
the paid hand." Birger paused, keeping his eyes on me. I
knew then why he had come to find me. He wasn't a very
intelligent man and he wanted help.

"But I know something," he said.

I was not watching the big man carefully then and I
may have missed something significant that he did, or said.
The room seemed to have grown still and tense, as I remember, while Birger was talking. I believe now that something happened in the pause after Birger said, "I'm only
the paid hand." In any event, I was suddenly aware that
the big man sitting on my left was idiotically humming to
himself, his protuberant eyes turned to the rafters. He began to sing words to a senseless sort of tune, mumbling
them and running them one into another. Birger was
watching him and listening. According to the song, daffo-
dils and daisies, buttercups and pinks were picked to build
a garden hut for stopping up the chinks. It was that sort of
song. I do not remember the actual words, but with each

verse more flowers came in, and suddenly Birger cried, "Stop!"

He put away his pistol and walked to the table and sat down. "I was in that garden myself," he said. "With two of them. Can you beat it? But I came from Oslo."

"Then you were with Moeller and Torgersen."

"Correct. I'm Croeger."

"Holter."

The two men shook hands, then the big fellow, Holter, looked at me. "We have something to discuss," he said. "If you would excuse us, please?"

I realized, of course, that these two had managed to convey to each other that they were of the Resistance movement. I was not really in it myself, only, as you might say, on the edge of it. I could have made up a little song using a dozen names, but I would never have risked doing so. I know what Nils would have had to say to me about trying a thing like that.

"Certainly," I agreed. "You can do what you like." If they were of the Resistance they were bound to be all right. I always knew Birger was a good chap—a woman's instinct. The learned may sneer, but I have found it to work time and time again. In fact, I have never made a serious error when trusting to my instinct.

"If you are a friend of Croeger's," Holter said to me, "you're safer here than in a lot of other places. There's nothing for you to be scared of."

Of course not—wasn't I having a nice quiet evening at home? "Do as you wish," I told him. He seemed to be in command.

"Then you won't mind if we leave you for a moment?"

"I'm leaving this house myself as soon as it is light enough for me to see my way."

"I wouldn't do that just yet," Holter said. "I wouldn't leave the house for a while. You're safer here. I think things are going to start up once it gets light and it won't be very healthy just at that time. And now—"

The two went out into the yard together to make their plans. I think they also went to keep an eye on the *Leonora,* but they had plenty to talk over. I found out later that Birger (Croeger) was in this business entirely from a private angle. He had been approached as a private citizen and offered a high wage to use his seafaring knowledge. I am convinced he knew nothing about the gold until it was on board, but then, being a Joessing, he developed an interest in the affair. Birger was a brave man.

Meanwhile I sat in my kitchen and waited for them to come back. I felt a good deal safer—having a man around the house makes a difference. Dawn was not far away. The night was very still, and I sat for some time turning the happenings of the last twenty-four hours over in my mind. It did not seem so fantastic now. I seemed to have become used to the idea of living on an improbable level of high adventure and I was more or less resigned to anything.

After I had made myself a cup of real tea and drunk it, I turned down the wick of the lamp and went out onto the veranda. The sky over the fjord was clear, full of a steely light in which the stars were pricked out like metallic flashes. In Norway the light never seems to fade right out of the sky. Even at midnight and in midwinter there is this steely echo of daylight on the other side of the world. The smell of the fjord was in my nostrils; the only sound that reached my ears was the rhythmic breathing of the surf below. The moon was high, shining behind a lacy flow of thin cloud and making shadows around the old house, sharp and clear-cut as if snipped out of the darkness of the night with scissors. Across the floor boards of the veranda the shadows lay as if pinned to the posts that supported the roof. The rest of the floor was washed with a silver light as remote and unreal as the moon itself.

You would have sworn that in this moonlit world nothing was stirring, that time had passed on leaving this silver-gray seascape far behind in space, but I was certain that aboard the *Leonora,* only a cable's length away in the darkness, two men were at work getting ready to sail. On shore, and in other places for all I knew, others were watching, listening for the splash of dropped moorings and the grind of starter motors.

I went back indoors. I had not been in the kitchen long before Birger came silently in, carrying a rifle. "Miss," he said. "Don't think we've been taking liberties, but there isn't much time left now. We've been looking around. Did you have more than one boat in the boathouse?"

"The little sailing dinghy," I told him. "The one with the sails and gear on the beams overhead."

"It's gone," Birger informed me. "Someone's been ashore to get it."

I must have looked blank, for he went on, "I came ashore in the *Leonora's* dinghy and this time I hid it properly. I didn't want them chasing after me. You see, Miss, I couldn't risk being picked up by the Quislings—if you understand? I lit out because I didn't like the risk. But it's different now."

"What's changed?" I asked.

"It's different. Anyway, they've got your sailing dinghy and that means they're off for where they're going to bury the gold. There's one thing, Miss. Did you hear anyone taking the gold off while you were aboard?"

"No."

"Think you would have heard?"

"Yes. I heard all of you come back and leave again. I heard Holter come aboard."

"And this place, Miss. Has anyone been around?"

"Only you two that I know of."

"You didn't notice if anyone had been in the cellars or the sheds?"

"I haven't looked at the sheds but I don't think anyone was in the house before I got here."

"He's still got the gold aboard, then. But he kept Erik and me separate. Neither knew what the other was doing. He's as wily as a fox, Miss. They may have a little trouble over the start, though."

"I should think they could manage without you now."

"I'm not thinking about that. Erik took the distributors out of the engines so no one could steal the boat while we were away, and I think he's lost a carbon brush or something. They were looking for it when I slipped off—His Lordship wasn't half raising cain!" He turned to the door, but I stopped him.

"That isn't one of the rifles from the boat, is it?"

He shook his head. "When I left I just wanted to drop quietly out of the picture. I wasn't looking for trouble."

"You didn't find the rifle here?"

"Oh, this!" He looked evasively away from me. "It belongs to Holter."

"I see. He has others, I suppose?"

"I couldn't tell you that, Miss. I wouldn't ask too many questions."

"You don't mind using my house, though."

"No harm will come to it, if we can help it. I wouldn't come wandering outdoors yet, Miss. You'll stay in?"

"I'll see."

15

THE FIGHT ON THE
JETTY

BIRGER left me. I heard his steps across the veranda, and from the kitchen window I saw him turn into the barn. This was a large building converted into a two-story structure, with part of the lower floor a garage. From the garage a ladder leads to the loft overlooking the end of the jetty on the shore side. It was beginning to get light now, and I realized that the two men were keeping watch on the *Leonora* from the window of the barn. It was a place that commanded the whole sweep of the channel.

As I watched over the flat stretch of sand beyond the wreckage of the old beachwall, I saw the first flame of the dawn touch the horizon on the hills. Soon it was light enough to see the distant white of the breakers as they rolled in to the shore; and before long the gulls came sailing up to patrol the wet sands left by the receding tide. The *Leonora* lay at her moorings with no sign of life aboard. It looked a peaceful scene, not so much the start of a new day as the start of a new world.

It came very suddenly. As I was scanning the islands to

seaward, there came a distant grating sound. It passed; but I knew that the *Leonora*'s engines were now turning over, and my heart began to beat with excitement. At any moment now I would see Erik or Jan himself cast off the buoy, and the *Leonora* would swing around to work up a feather at her prow. Jan would never dream I was still in the house; probably he thought I had lost no time getting back to Oslo, and Birger the same.

For an age nothing at all seemed to happen on the *Leonora,* then Erik came on deck and moved forward. He untied the boat and ran back to drop into the cockpit.

As the *Leonora* swung away I saw that my dinghy was being towed behind her. Then, at the moment Erik dropped, a shot rang out—almost in my ear it seemed. A splinter of wood flaked off the deck, and I caught a glimpse of Erik's face as he jerked his head around, then disappeared.

Three shots followed the first from the barn. It was impossible to see whether they scored hits, but the effect was dramatic. At first I thought Jan was heading the boat around to make the beach and fight it out ashore, for the *Leonora* came to port in a tight circle, but just off the end of the jetty she circled again and I realized Holter or Birger—or whoever else was in my barn—had made a lucky, or a very skillful, hit.

We did not have long to wait for Jan's reply. A succession of shots tore the air, followed by the whine of ricochets from the rocks. You could hear the bullets whacking into the wood of the barn. The turning course of the boat unsighted the men in the cockpit, and before they could fire again, Holter or Birger let *Leonora* have it. I don't think

I had time to be truly frightened. It was thrilling, something like a film, a riot of bangs and crashes.

It was clear the rudder lines had gone or the rudder itself was damaged, because the *Leonora* now was steering on her throttles. Even so, she could not hold a course, as the rudder was jammed over too hard. The battle, Jan must have realized, was too one-sided. A boat is more vulnerable than a two-hundred-year-old barn, and the *Leonora* was taking terrific punishment. The glass screening of the cockpit was milk-colored where bullets had splintered it, and her hull must have been riddled. Behind her rode my dinghy, saucy and untouched.

I think I had known all along what Jan would do. He opened up on the starboard engine as the *Leonora* came around toward the jetty, which for a moment pulled her straighter on her course. I thought she would miss by inches, but she did not miss. She crashed into the piling and thrust half her length among the planks. For a while the engine ran on, sending back a swirl of mud and sand, then they cut and Jan came on deck, slowly and deliberately, as if he were sampling the early morning air.

I shall never forget the sight of him that gray morning with the light strengthening about him as he stood. The sweep of the fjord made a vast, impersonal background of neutral tone. On the far horizon the hills were etched sharply above the halftones of the water. That strange peace still seemed to hang over everything now the tornado of shooting had ceased. Jan's left shoulder was red with blood and I could see that it came from the back of his head, for his neck was shiny with blood, too. He had a handkerchief tied around his forearm, stained crimson.

He wore a leather belt with two holsters and cradled in his arms was a rifle.

He stepped carefully up onto the jetty and I could see he was watching the window of the barn. Then, as in a nightmare, I saw him begin to walk along those planks. I wanted to call out to him, "Go back! Go *back*, Jan! They'll kill you!" But I could not speak. The muscles of my throat had contracted. I could hardly breathe. Jan was going to be killed, and I did not want him to die.

It seemed to me that his unhurried advance continued for a long time, but it could only have been a few paces before a shot rang out from the barn. They were firing straight down the length of the jetty, a target that could not be missed. I saw Jan flung back. He twisted as he fell, and I heard the thud of his rifle hitting the planking. I turned away. There was an angry thought in my head that this was not fair, shooting him again when he had already been hit twice.

I did not know it then, but Erik was dead. He had been hit through the mouth and killed instantly in the first burst from the barn, and Jan had to drop his rifle and take up the steering. Birger was also hit in the first exchange. Part of his left hand—the hand with which he was cradling his Remington—was taken away by a bullet, but Holter tied a rope around his arm above the elbow and Birger went on shooting.

Now they had killed Jan. I had a wild impulse to run out and cross into the barn, crying, "Stop! You've killed him! Isn't that enough?"

Quiet again over the channel. The gulls were sailing by unperturbed, the breakers were rolling in, the huddled

figure lying on the planks did not move. I could see the
blood spreading over the wood. . . .

Then Jan rolled over and his good arm stretched out.
He was on his haunches—now he was up. He picked up the
rifle and began walking forward again. You might have
thought he had merely tripped himself up and recovered.
A shot crashed out from the barn and I heard the whine
of a ricochet over the water. Jan lifted his gun and fired
back. He had difficulty in working the ejector and for a
moment he stood stock-still, tugging at it. "Lie down," I
wanted to scream. "Let them think you are dead! Go back
to the boat!" With all my heart I was willing him to drop
into the sea—anything but to walk pigheadedly on to get
at the men who were shooting at him.

But he was moving forward once more. He was shooting from the hip, and I could hear the bullets smacking
into the barn. I could see the splinters fly around the window. And all the time he kept advancing. "The next shot,"
I was thinking. "The next shot will get him. They'll kill
him before he reaches the end."

Holter was still firing from the window, though blinded
in one eye from a splinter. Birger was dead; a bullet had
struck him in the cheek and taken half his face away. There
was no back of his head at all.

As far as I can remember it, Jan Goffinger fired as he
came along the whole length of the jetty. When he neared
the end the return fire from the barn ceased. Holter was
finished too. . . .

Jan stopped firing. I can see him now as he stood looking
up at the barn. A froth of blood was blowing out and suck-
ing back into his mouth. His face was chalk-white in the

early light. One ankle bone was grotesquely twisted and his shoe full of blood. He seemed to be treading on the side of that foot and he was swaying like a drunken man, but fight was burning like a flame in him. Distantly I heard him shouting out something at the barn, but no answer came. He shouted for a while, then I saw him turn and wobble back down the jetty.

I believe now that if Jan Goffinger had been mortally wounded he would not have been able to do what he did do in those last minutes. I do not think he was a dying man. In any event, he staggered back to the boat, leaving a trail of blood behind him, and managed to heave himself onto the deck. I stood transfixed on the veranda, trying to make myself believe that he had walked up to the barn and back.

How long I was there staring at the *Leonora* I do not know. There is no means of telling, for I was in another world where time does not count. All I can say now is that I remember hearing the engines of the *Leonora* start up. The boat eased herself out of the wreckage at the end of the jetty and began to head into the fjord. She was no longer on a circular course. She seemed to be steering, and she steered out into the fjord.

That was the last I saw of her. It was the last anyone ever saw of the *Leonora*.

16

BODIES IN THE BARN

IT TOOK time for the spell to break and for me to realize where I was that morning, and what had been happening. It was still early dawn. The world around me was still slowly weakening, oblivious of the tremendous events that had been shattering its peace. The gulls were still slow-winging along the beach, and the breakers traced their leisurely mile-wide rolling to the shore. I seemed to come out of one state very sharply into another, as if projected by some outside force. I was thinking: This can't still be going on just as if nothing has happened!

But it was, the background of distant murmuring from the breakers, the feel of the wind, the reassuring scent of the pines were there. Not a soul was to be seen, nor was there any sign of human movement in the whole wide sweep from hills to sea. No sight or sound of life from the barn.

Holter had warned me not to move out of the house, but I thought that whatever had been going to happen had already happened. So I hurried along the veranda, down the steps, and over the stone flags to the garage. "Birger! Birger!" I called out as I climbed the ladder to the loft. "It's me!"—still possessing enough sense to realize I might be met with bullets.

No one answered me. As my head drew level with the floor boards above, the terrible reek of blood—of gaping flesh wounds—hit me like a blow in the face. There is nothing like it. The scent is not the sort of odor that could be connected with blood by inference. It had a cloying, sickly sweet background and the nearest approach to it I can think of is the smell you get when pulling the skin off a dead rabbit. I began to retch as I stepped into the loft.

Birger had been thrown back in a sprawling heap with his limbs buckled under him in a way that said quite clearly he was dead. It was as if a bundle of something had been carelessly tossed away in a corner. Apart from this, his neck appeared to end in a heap of scarlet gravel. I was caught up by convulsions of nausea then. I never looked at that "head" again. I daren't.

When I recovered I walked over to the apple racks that by some freak had caught Holter's arm when he fell. The big man was half hanging on the rack and half sprawled on the floor. His face was dead-white, quite bloodless except for a crimson sweep on one cheek and the neck. His mouth gaped wide and his undamaged eye was wide, too, with a great deal of the white showing from under a lowered lid. His limbs were buckled under him and a rifle was trapped between his thighs. He looked like a fowl that had its throat cut—a fowl that had bled to death, white and flabby. I forced myself to put my hand over his heart. There was no trace of a beat. So Holter was dead too.

There was one thing only I wanted then, to get out and stay away. Only to try to forget those corpses. Yet even to-day I remember what I saw in that loft—the memory will suddenly spring back on me for no reason at all at any moment, during a piece of music, or in the middle of a conversation, when I have not thought of Larkollen for months —and I will recall that sweet smell of death and the blood-less body of Holter, with its single staring eye.

But there was something that had to be attended to first: I had to cover the bodies. The instinct was strong. I suppose it lies at the bottom of the age-old custom of burial of the dead. In some intimate way the human mind shrinks from the thought of leaving the body of one of its kind exposed, and a psychologist might say that a body covered up is already halfway dismissed from consciousness. The mind does not like to admit that a thing like death exists. Shakily I managed to get down the ladder and over the stone flags, returning to the house through the kitchen. I went up to my linen cupboard and hunted two of my oldest sheets (the housewife instinct is also very strong). I did not grab the first sheets in the cupboard, but sorted them carefully in a mechanical sort of way, my real thoughts elsewhere.

As I made my way down the stairs again into the hall, a sudden scrape in the yard halted me as if a movie of what was happening had suddenly been stopped. Steps sounded on the stones and someone pushed at the kitchen door, which swung inward. I must have made some sort of terri-fied noise, for the steps hurried nearer and a voice called out in a country dialect, "Fru Astrup! *Er det noen hjemme? Er det noe paa faerde?*"

Was I there! Was there anything wrong! Then, suddenly I recognized the voice. The relief when I peeped through the rails and saw buxom, red-cheeked Siri Voss peering anxiously about my kitchen! Siri's widowed mother ran the post office at the village, and Siri, whom I had known since she was a baby, delivered the mail.

"I'm here, Siri," I called out. I managed to get down the remaining stairs and walk into the kitchen. I realized then that the scraping noise I had heard was the well-known sound of the girl's bicycle.

"So you're back," Siri said. "I thought someone screamed when I knocked at the door."

"You must have imagined it." I felt I must hide what I knew about the corpses in my loft. "I'm just leaving. Don't deliver any more letters here because—because I shan't be here, Siri. Do you understand?"

I am sure now she could see something was very wrong from the way I was talking. Anyone with any intelligence would have seen it—even poor Siri, who believed, as did her mother, in the trolls. But Siri had sensational news of her own on her mind.

"It is not letters I am delivering to you, Fru Astrup. I came out the day before yesterday but could make no one hear. There was no smoke and no car and the boat—"

"There was no one here, Siri." I wished that she would just leave the letters or circulars or whatever she had, and go.

"A telegram came for you on Monday, then another this morning, and my mother said to me, 'Siri, you must take your cycle and go out to Fru Astrup's at Larkollen. For here is another of them. The same words and it must be urgent.' "

She fumbled in the leather wallet she carried in her

little sack and handed me two telegrams. As I took them—
how distinctly one can recall every detail of such scenes!—
I was saying to myself angrily, "That Nils!" I thought he
was poking his nose into my affairs again, trying to find
where I had gone. I had an idea from the first that he saw
through my story of going to see the farmers for food. Suddenly, I asked myself, "Why two telegrams?"

"Aren't you going to open them?" Siri demanded.

Then, mercifully, she spared me reading the message
first in cold print. The shock was lessened because although
I heard what she said distinctly I had a thought at the back
of my head that she did not really know what was inside,
that a simple girl like Siri would not know what she was
talking about anyway. What she said was, "It is about
Kirsti, Fru Astrup."

I tore open the first telegram and read, "COME AT ONCE
KIRSTI ILL HJOERDIS." Mechanically I opened the second
telegram and read exactly the same message. I can see the
girl's face now, staring up at me, bovine and scared. "Was
there any other message, Siri?" I asked her.

"No, Fru Astrup. Will there be an answer?"

I thought for a moment. Sister Hjoerdis obviously must
have been sending telegrams to every place where I might
be. Probably she was still trying to find me. There had to
be an answer, although I did not want everyone to know
where I had been for the last two days. I wrote a reply that
I was coming and sent it to Sister Hjoerdis at the hospital.
Then Siri got on her bicycle and left.

Kirsti ill! For them to send two wires, she must be seriously ill. Perhaps she was not expected to live? Perhaps she
was dead already? My usual panic was working up. Perhaps she had asked for me, waited for me to come? I was

standing by my desk, still clutching the bed sheets, staring at nothing. I was telling myself: "You get yourself mixed up in an affair like this . . . and now you will never see Kirsti again."

But soon reason began to get the upper hand. The pendulum swung back, and something said, "Dead? Who said she was dead? Probably she has mumps and is howling the place down. Of course they would want you there. It may be a tonsillectomy and they would have to have your consent, wouldn't they?"

I stared at the sheets. For a while I could not imagine what I would be doing with sheets—old ones, too. Then it came back to me. There were two dead men in the loft.

It never occurred to me that people might ask why I did not mention the dead men to Siri. It never struck me that putting my sheets over them would probably connect me with the affair. I carried the sheets up to the barn and shut my nostrils against the stench. I tried to rearrange Birger's limbs, but the leg of a corpse is a much heavier thing than you imagine. I could do little with the body, so I left Birger as he was and draped a sheet over him. Then I turned to the body of Holter.

With this one, I had to unhook the arm from the rack. I shrank from touching the corpse. I tried not to look at its staring eye. I tugged at the shoulder and prized at the wrist. Suddenly the whole cadaver collapsed, and, turning, slid toward the door. The shoulder levered itself on the edge of the rack and the arm came up and over, letting the hand fall on my neck. It was as if the dead man were reaching for me.

This time I really let go. I heard my scream echoing back and forth among the farm buildings and it would not have surprised me if they had heard it far out at sea. I realized I was screaming, and I wanted to stop; but I went on screaming all the same and I did not stop until I had rolled over the boards and disentangled myself from the dead man's arm.

I left the sheet on the floor and ran. I have no recollection of touching the rungs of the ladder as I dropped to the garage; the next thing I can clearly remember is washing my hands and my face and the back of my neck and scrubbing them with a towel.

The kettle was giving up a plume of steam on the stove. I had to get back to Dilling, to get the train, and I had to get there as quickly as possible. Panic would not help me. I had had no breakfast that morning. I made a pot of tea and drank a cup, then decided to be brave and go back to cover up the body of poor Holter. It was the least I could do for him. I returned to the barn.

The body looked ghastly on the boards. It looked like someone who had been surprised by death and was rather hurt about it all. A splinter of wood had been knocked out of Holter's scalp by his new fall and there seemed to be more blood about. The bottom of his trousers had been concertinaed up to his knees. I straightened his legs and began to pull his trousers down before covering him with the sheet—

But I never got far with the laying out of the corpse. My body became numb with an actual feeling of intense cold. The man beside my knees *had moved.*

Holter was dead. I had felt for a heartbeat and there was none. How could a dead man move, except by some reflex action? Nerves and my imagination. . . . Who could wonder after all I had been through that day?

Holter suddenly drew up his legs and sat up. For a while he stared at me blankly. Then his gaze gradually focused and took life. "Fru Astrup. . . ." he said. His voice was hoarse and he had to moisten his lips before he could manage the words. But he smiled at me. "The little bird!"

"I—I thought you were dead," I managed. The relief of hearing him talk made me feel hysterical. He was human! He was living! I could have hugged him.

"What's been going on around here? What's happened to me?" Holter looked around, then seemed to remember. "I must have taken the count. Something hit me when that chap was coming along the jetty. . . . And you were going to cover me decently with one of your sheets? Well, I'm not sorry to say I shall disappoint you! I don't think I'm badly hurt." He had one hand pressed to the side of his scalp. "I think I've stopped bleeding. Perhaps if—"

"Stay where you are! I'll fetch bandages and iodine and water."

"I'll come with you." He turned to look at the heap under the sheet beside him, and said slowly, "It happened in the first exchange. We got the man at the helm, then—"

I helped Holter to his feet. The color was coming back into his face, but he still looked far from healthy. He was able to walk and I managed to get him down the ladder and out of the loft.

"The boat?" he suddenly asked.

"He reversed his engines and got her off. He took her out into the fjord. I think he was badly wounded. I think he was far gone."

For some time he said nothing; then he asked me quietly, "Have you seen anyone around the place?"

I told him about Siri and that I had not let her know anything about the fight, or what was in the barn.

He walked shakily across the yard to the kitchen, where I bathed his wound. He did not seem inclined to say much, but he warned me not to touch the cut in his scalp as scalp wounds bleed easily and profusely.

"Make a round bandage and leave it as it is," he said.

"I have to go. I have to see my daughter. I don't like to leave you like this."

"Someone will be along," Holter told me. "I'm all right. Run along, and I hope your little girl is well by now."

"But—"

"Everything will be taken care of here. I think you understand? There are plenty of us around here."

"I understand."

"For the moment do not talk. Not to anyone."

"I understand."

"All right. Now go."

I left Holter sitting by the stove. The rest of his party who had been after the *Leonora* would pick him up soon enough. They would bury Birger and tidy up the place. The house no longer seemed to belong to me. I now had a strong antipathy toward it, for it seemed alien and hostile. "Let them have it," I thought. "Let them do what they like with the place." I wondered if the rest of them had managed to catch up with Jan. . . .

I pulled on my gloves and my coat and walked out of the house, through the yard and garden, and down the valley path at the back on the way to Dilling.

17

HOME TO KIRSTI

I HAD a two hours' walk to reach the railway, and it was not until I was nearly there that I met anyone. Just before Dilling station I got a lift in a countryman's cart. Delicate sparring between us produced the information that this farmer was not a Nazi sympathizer, so I told him I had no permit to be out of Oslo and perhaps not enough money to get back there. I told him who I was and where I lived at Larkollen. He gave me twenty kroner and took me to the station where he himself talked with the stationmaster, who was a friend of his. This official insisted on giving me a ticket free of charge, so I insisted on returning the twenty kroner to my phlegmatic farmer-friend.

I had a long wait for the train, but no one asked questions when I got aboard. Even on the country trains passengers did not talk among themselves to any extent in Norway at that time. The country was too sharply divided, and you never knew whether your neighbor was a Quisling or an honest Joessing. You kept your mouth shut and minded your own business. The train was terribly slow, and before long I realized it was going to be a near thing whether I got into Oslo before the curfew. Delay followed delay at wayside stations, and soon I knew it was hopeless.

When the train eventually drew into East Station it was nearer ten o'clock than nine, so I resigned myself as best I might to spending the night in a waiting room. I avoided the Germans on the platform and made my way across the hall to the telephone booths, where I called the hospital. "A slight operation for removing the tonsils," I kept saying. "Mumps, measles, chicken pox. A slight operation for removing the tonsils. . . ."

A voice suddenly said, "Ullevaal Hospital."

I swallowed and tried to control my reply. "Alexandra Ward, please. Sister Hjoerdis."

"Hold on." It seemed an age before anyone answered in the ward, then a young voice said, "Alexandra Ward."

"Can I—I speak to Sister Hjoerdis, please?"

"Who is it?"

"The mother of a patient."

"Sister Hjoerdis is on day duty. She went off duty at six. What name is it?"

News of Kirsti was the one thing I wanted in all the world, but I dreaded that if I gave my name this young nurse would say, "But your daughter died this morning, Fru Astrup." I could not risk hearing that awful thing. I said quickly, before the nurse could tell me anything, "It doesn't matter," and hung up.

I found another ten öre and rang up my apartment, hoping Hjoerdis might be at home. I heard the bell ringing—or the signal that meant it was ringing—in my sitting room, and I could imagine the telephone there by the window, by the row of books with the elephant book ends. She would have to come from her bedroom—perhaps the ringing was wakening the girls sleeping after duty, and it would take time for them to—

A voice cut in; I recognized it at once. It was Olga, a young probationer from Stavanger. "Olga," I said, "this is Fru Astrup. I must speak to Sister Hjoerdis. I must—I. . . ." I had to know, so I blurted out, "My Kirsti. Is she—"

"Hjoerdis is not here yet, Fru Astrup."

"Kirsti!" I said.

"She's all right. Still under observation. Sister Hjoerdis has been telegraphing trying to get hold of you for—"

"Then she's not dead?"

"Of course not."

"Observation? Observation for what?" I wanted to dance. To rush out into the station and tell someone. Anyone. Even a policeman. "You see," something was saying inside me, "she isn't dead. Never any question of it. Just your panic."

"She was asking for you all the time, so Sister Hjoerdis—"

This was not so good, but I still felt buoyed up. "What are the symptoms?"

"Sickness. Cannot take food. Headache and stiffness of the neck."

Polio! I knew then that she was going to die after all. Weren't these the symptoms? Would Sister Hjoerdis have sent two wires for measles?

"She came in from Fru Wiik's on Monday and Sister Hjoerdis wasn't satisfied. There was no reason for the tem-

perature to keep up. No rashes. So she put her in the observation ward and she's there now, Fru Astrup."

"I want to see her but I'm at the East Station."

"Don't risk coming here without a pass. I'll tell Sister
Hjoerdis you called when she comes in. The little girl
wouldn't know you. Don't come until the morning."

"I won't come until morning," I promised. "Don't forget to tell Hjoerdis. . . ."

There were some dozen travelers stranded in that cheer-
less waiting room. It was impossible for me to rest. My
thoughts tortured me and I stared at the framed photographs of Norwegian beauty spots that adorned the walls
until I was sick of the sight of them. A woman beside me
was snoring. Two young men were playing cards, slapping
the cards down in the way peasants play. A very old man,
obviously from the mountains, sat, like me, staring at nothing. I wondered what was in his mind.

I thought: Nearly two hours gone now. Seven more to
wait. I did not see how I was ever going to get through
them. Then the swinging door opened and a man came in.
The newcomer looked around as if searching for a comfortable seat, then let himself down near the door and
stretched his arms, yawning. After a while he appeared to
remember something and left the room again. After a decent interval I left too. Nils was waiting in the shadows. He
gripped my arm.

There are very few people in this world I respect as I
respected Nils. Perhaps he was a man without culture or
education, but he was sincere, honest, and as trustworthy as
humans are made. I would have done a great deal for Nils
if at any time he was in need. He did a great deal for me.

"Kirsti is all right," he said. "Don't worry about her. Hjoerdis got your message. She's glad her wire reached you and that you're back. She's been on to me only just now and Kirsti is all right."

"She has a persistent temperature," I said, unconvinced.

"Children often have persistent temperatures. If Hjoerdis says she's all right, what more do you want?"

"I want to see her," I told him sharply.

"What do you think I'm here for? Of course you want to see her. Although it didn't look like it in the last few days."

"Nils," I said. "Nils—I've been away. I've got something to tell you."

"It can wait. You can't begin your confessions in the middle of East Station. I have a car in the yard outside. We're all right as long as we're not searched. And we're not going to be. It's a German staff car."

"I want to tell you something important," I said.

"Later. We shall have a lot of time waiting at the hospital. In the morgue—remember?"

"I remember." I started moving and as we went I said to him, "Nils, I want to ask you something about our group. About us."

"Not here," he told me.

We walked into the baggage office and Nils opened the flap in the counter. The clerk there had a shade over his eyes. He was reading a paper-backed novel, his feet on the stove, and must have been expecting us, for he never looked up. Nils led the way through the back room and we got into a little gray-painted car. We seemed to fly through the deserted streets; soon were in the yard I remembered so well, at the Ullevaal Hospital.

"Well, that was all right," Nils said. He faced me sternly. "Now you can tell me what's on your mind. I *knew* you were up to something when I saw you with the *vaktmester* that evening. Well—what is it?"

It is a strange thing that so complex and well-organized an institution as the Resistance could operate in the almost complete darkness in which it worked. Each little cell only knew its own members. You knew the man above and the man below and no one else. This was for safety, of course, for the Gestapo had drugs and other means to make men talk, and no one can talk of things he does not know. Nils, it turned out, had no knowledge of Birger–Croeger or Holter or any of the group that had been chasing the *Leonora*. Neither he nor any of our little group had any means of knowing. Yet Nils's own name had been mentioned by Holter in his flower song. (Nils's underground name would have started a fight in any English bar; it was "Pansy"!) Two other Oslo Resistance men had also been mentioned by Holter, but nevertheless what I had to say came as a complete surprise to Nils.

In the mortuary, while waiting for news of Kirsti, I started at the beginning and told Nils everything. He heard me out in silence, then asked me a lot of questions about Jan—when I had first met him, what he used to talk about, what he seemed to be interested in, how well I knew him. It was easy for me to answer whether I had ever in any way —even the smallest—been indiscreet about our part of the movement.

"Nils," I said, "I have never at any time told anyone

anything. So I know he could not have got any information out of me—if he had such a thing in mind."

"What was the name Holter asked you about when he first came on you?"

"Goerdler."

Nils turned it over in his mind. At length he said, "I don't know what he had to do with it, whoever he may be. They seemed to expect to meet a chap called Goerdler, eh? Well, I imagine I can get a line on him if I ask someone. . . . You seem to have had quite a time. Some of our chaps down there, it seems. It wants thinking over. Goerdler? Goerdler—I ought to know that name."

The old Jewish man, Hitchman, came in with mugs of coffee, and brought me hospital buns and some sandwiches which I appreciated, for I had had nothing to eat all day. Shortly after this Nils spoke on the house telephone to the ward and reported to me that Kirsti was sleeping. There was nothing more than that.

"Hjoerdis is at your place," he said. "When she comes on duty in the morning we'll get the latest news."

"Nils," I said. "I've been through a lot in the last days, but I'm not afraid to face up to things. It is polio—isn't it? Why can't they tell me? It's not knowing that gets me down. It's polio, isn't it?"

To my relief he was puzzled. "I've not heard the name. What is it? Hjoerdis certainly never said it."

"Infantile paralysis."

"No one has said that. I'm sure they would have said if it had been infantile paralysis. She's been in the hospital three days. She's—her movements are all right."

"Nils," I said; my heart went out to him. "You've been in to see her?"

"Naturally, for as long as she could recognize me. I told her you were coming."

I could have hugged him, but instead I stupidly began to cry. The surroundings were not cheerful. For some reason only low-power bulbs were used down in the mortuary, perhaps to create an appropriate funereal atmosphere. The walls were painted chocolate and the air was cold and had the smell of death in it. The little room in which we were sitting had a common deal table and three hard chairs, a calendar from an undertaker on the wall, and nothing else at all. There was no sound except our low-pitched conversation.

"Are we all right in this place, Nils?"

"Safe enough. Especially after daylight. Anyway, I have a right to be here. We service this place."

I could not at first think what he meant, then I remembered that they must have refrigerators in a mortuary. And I had a child in the hospital, hadn't I? "I want to see Hjoerdis. I want to hear all about it."

"You will hear in the morning."

We sat out the rest of the night together, Nils and I, and in the morning someone sent down two trays with our breakfast. Later Hjoerdis came down. She seemed relieved to see me. "I can't stay long," she told me. "Come back in visiting hours this afternoon at four. I'll have more news for you then. She's all right. No worse."

"What happened?" I asked her.

"Fru Wiik phoned that Kirsti was sick and didn't want to eat. I sent the ambulance on the chance, and when she got here I saw at once she was ill. She had a temperature, but the doctor did not seem to know what it was."

"Polio?"

"I don't think so. There are the pains in the neck, of course. Yet the other symptoms . . . not quite."

"But she's delirious!"

"That's the fever and persistent temperatures. She's well looked after and everything is being done."

"I know. I know. But—"

"You'll see her for yourself this afternoon.

She looked at me. "Well, I must go. If I were you, I would get back home. It's about time you got back. Where on earth have you been? Where did you go?"

"Larkollen."

"I wired everywhere. I had a hell of a time! Why didn't you tell anyone you were going?"

"Hjoerdis," I said, "I'm sorry. I'll be telling you soon."

"There's nothing you can do waiting here—and you really shouldn't be here, you know."

This was the official attitude coming out in Hjoerdis, but I saw her point. Nils took me home and promised to call later in the day after I had slept. Strangely enough, I did manage to get some sleep. I lay on the bed trying to think and the next I knew it was three-thirty in the afternoon and Nils was—once more—sitting on the end of my bed.

He had a startling story to tell me.

18

GOERDLER

I COULD see Nils was wrought up about something. He is not an excitable type, but as he sat there on the end of my bed watching me, an unusual tenseness in his face struck me at once. "Look," he said. "Before I say anything to you—before we begin to talk and you get other subjects in your mind that may suggest things—just imagine you are looking at a magazine and you see this. What would you say?"

He pulled out a large envelope and handed me a piece of paper, which I took still only half-awake. "Have you heard from the hospital, Nils?" I asked him. The paper was a folder, and inside was a glossy photographic print, rather blurred. It showed some men standing in a room with a mantelpiece and fireplace that looked vaguely French.

"You can go in and see her at five o'clock. I shall take you. Hjoerdis says there is nothing to report. But the picture—well?"

"Is she still delirious?" The only thing I knew about

fever is that it is weakening. The longer it lasts the more likely you are to lose the fight.

"She's taken some black-currant juice. But look at the photo. That's an actual print. Do you see anything?"

I felt there were more important things to discuss than our own little photographic efforts in the group. One of our members—Anders Dahl, a chemist with a shop in Rosenkrantzgaten—was a miniature-camera expert, and he had fitted up a darkroom which we used for copying documents and developing microfilm.

"I see the graining. It is not a good enlargement and shouldn't have been blown up to this size. Who are the men? Germans? Important Nazis?"

Nils nodded, keeping his eyes on mine. "Germans. Now take another look."

I swung my legs off the bed and switched on the reading light. Two of the men in the picture looked like generals out of uniform; in fact, that was what they are. One of them was von Rundstedt, and the other some lesser general whose name I have now forgotten. A tall, spare man, also in civilian clothes, was standing slightly to one side of the generals and looking in their direction, and you somehow got the impression that he was included in the group because he was an adjutant or aide and his general had said, "Come on in, Colonel. I want you in this, too."

"Is something planned—for them?" I asked. This sort of print was occasionally used when people were going out to liquidate Germans, Quislings, or other traitors, so as to avoid mistakes.

"Nothing is planned. Well, you do not recognize anyone?"

The natural result of a question like this is, of course, that you take a second and more interested look. If you feel you ought to know someone in the picture your reaction is different. I had not the slightest indication before Nils said "recognize," but the moment he spoke that word I discovered Jan Goffinger as the third man in the picture. Though he looked younger and different, the "aide" might have been Jan. It was a poor picture, though; you couldn't be certain.

"No, I don't recognize anyone," I said.

"You have never seen any of those men before?"

"Never."

He took the folder back and tucked it away in a portfolio he was carrying. "Well, I've got to talk to you . . . and this is important. Try to think clearly and don't say you remember anything that you don't clearly remember, because once you have said you remember something, you remember 'remembering' it, and not the thing itself, and so you get to be convinced of things you shouldn't be certain about at all."

"For heaven's sake, Nils!" I said.

"It makes sense if you think about it. And it will make more sense in a minute when I read you something you ought to know. I've been digging things up all day and it's very interesting, I can tell you. You knew Goffinger before the war?"

I told Nils where I had met Jan and when.

"Did you ever meet any Dutchman while he was with you? Did you hear him speaking Dutch with them?"

"I very seldom was with anyone else while I was with him." I considered for a minute, as Nils had told me to. "I don't think I can ever remember being with anyone else except Kirsti when Jan visited me, or took me out. He came mostly for lessons. But Jan was Dutch. I've seen his passport."

"Maybe. And after the Germans marched in and the BBC began their special broadcasts, he used to ask what the 'English' news was, didn't he?"

"He knew I was English."

"Never mind what he knew—he used to ask you about BBC news?"

I nodded, and of what I added I was quite certain. "I told him I never heard what the BBC said. I said—as I always did—that I had no means of knowing. Jan never pressed me further."

"He asked you about me that night we were on the streetcar?"

"He reproved me for being out so late. He—he didn't like the look of you. You were in workman's clothes, Nils," I added quickly.

"He asked questions about me?"

"No."

"You told him nothing about me?"

"Of course I said nothing. Except that you were an acquaintance, a man my husband had known."

"Certain?"

"Absolutely sure. I have never spoken about anyone. If you aren't clever and have to be close as an oyster, then at least you can be certain you have never said anything indiscreet."

"He told you plenty, though. He told you how he

spent his life in various countries, going about Europe with apparently nothing to do. What was his profession?"

"He—he never said. I always thought he had private means, was independent."

"He has funds in various countries?"

"Yes."

"And wanted to improve his languages. Don't you see where all this points?"

I did not answer. Nils was trying to make him out to be an international agent, a professional spy, the type who haunts the chancelleries of Europe—the counterpart of the glamorous woman spy of fiction. "It's nonsense," I said.

"Well, I can tell you something about Mr. Goffinger, and you are going to have a shock."

I was thinking: How ridiculous! All men are jealous of each other, particularly when a more or less helpless woman is concerned. She is like a bone thrown to two dogs. "More pictures?" I asked him sweetly.

He handed me a folder with a perfectly clear photograph of Jan's cousin, the young widow whose husband had been killed in Poland. "I know this one, of course," I said.

"Do you?" Nils turned the print over, and on the back was posted a typewritten slip. He pointed to it and said, "This is the woman he has been living with. Irma Sulzberger, wife of a German officer formerly employed at the German Embassy in Madrid. She has a dossier in quite a few centers interested in counterespionage."

You might have thought this would sound outrageous to me, who had believed the woman to be Jan's cousin, but as soon as Nils mentioned it I realized that part of me had known all along that Irma was his mistress.

"What does that prove?" I asked him. I was beginning to have a deep-seated, sick feeling. Part of the world I knew and trusted was crumbling away.

"Nothing, unless you begin to add everything up and look at the total, not the various figures. This chap had plenty of gold—so had all the top-level Nazis. He always seemed to know the movements of the Germans—he told you not to worry about the English air raid, didn't he? He seemed to have plenty of tobacco and drink and food, only available in two places—the black market and the German messes. Top ones, at that."

I did not know what to say.

"I'm coming to something that will explain why I'm going over all this first," Nils continued.

"I wish you would make it a little quicker and less mysterious. If you know something important why don't you come out with it?"

"You'll soon see. I had to follow all this up from just the mention of the name Goerdler."

"Well? I'm sure I don't know anything about *him*."

"Goerdler is the man with the generals in the picture you've just been looking at. Johan Joachim Albrecht Goerdler. That's not guesswork. It's in the records with his fingerprints and everything. Goerdler became a German Foreign Office attaché, and a lot of people would like to know more about that particular job of his. I'm talking about prewar—of our Norwegian secret service and doubtless lots of others. Most of what I have been looking at today has come from our own official Foreign Office files, together with some later ones from the police, and from our own records in the Resistance. Both Goerdler and the woman have dossiers here at the *Utenriksdepartement*."

"Why is all this so important now that he must be dead?" I heard myself ask. The feeling of living through something in which I could not believe grew stronger. It didn't seem like Nils telling me all this. I couldn't believe it was me listening.

"I'm coming to that. I expect you must have wondered what all the fuss was over him trying to slip out to sea. Dozens of small craft manage it every month."

"Well—yes. I didn't like the seaplane searching for us. It must have been a Resistance pilot—was it?"

"I expect it was," Nils said. "We were after him sure enough. He never had a chance to get away. You have been lucky again. Very, very lucky. You should never have been mixed up in that affair. You could have been blown up, or riddled with machine-gun bullets. Our people were not playing."

"Our people?"

"Not the group. Higher up than that. They weren't sure he was Goerdler but they were after him all right. You bet! You'll soon know why."

"Well, why don't you tell me?"

"When you have answered my last questions out of a clear mind, I will." He rolled himself a cigarette and lit it. "Think back. Did he ever tell you anything about gold— I mean, besides those cases? Or any bank accounts? Any box he might have in a strong room? Where he had got those cases from?"

"He never said where they came from and he took great pains to keep the information even from Birger and the

Dutchman Erik, his crew. He told me he had money in Spain and in South America but he did not say how or where. He never mentioned gold in this connection but I have a key of a strongbox he has at the Aker Sparebank here in Oslo and also I know the password for it."

Nils crushed his cigarette and jumped to his feet. "You *do?*" His eyes were hard and his keenness scared me a little. Something else seemed to have exploded in my face.

"I have the key and the password is Helsingfors." I crossed to my dressing table and unlocked my jewel case. I held up the key.

"What on earth did he give you the key for?"

"In case anything happened to him I was to go to the bank and get the contents of the box he had in the strong room. Why is all this so important?"

"Well! We'll certainly have a look in that box. And it may be most important. But not now." He took a sheet from his portfolio and opened it gravely. "I'm going to read you our report on something that happened in the first week after the Germans came to Oslo. Then you will see whether it is important or not. There is only one more question, Helen. I'm sorry but I have to ask all these things first."

"All right." I looked at my watch—half an hour before we would have to leave to go and see Kirsti at the hospital.

"The raid on Bugge next door here which ended in fiasco ... you didn't ring up anyone? Or make any mention in any way to anyone why you could not come out? Why you had to stay in?"

"Meaning—Jan Goffinger?"

"Meaning anyone at all."

"I did not telephone to anyone or see anyone except the men themselves and you."

Nils looked away. "If that chap is Goerdler—well, my dear, he used to come here quite a lot. Some of our people think he must have been Goerdler, and that he was responsible for that little business."

"I see." I was beginning to feel angry then.

"You will see more in a minute. But let me say first that I don't think Goerdler could have had anything to do with it. It was just bad luck that *Arkitekt* Hagen chanced to see what was happening. I'm sure myself, though, that your friend Jan and Goerdler are the same man. I believe he had a job as go-between—a kind of liaison between the Nazis here and the Quislings."

Nils smoothed out the sheet and began to read to me; it went like this.*

On the night of April 12, Gustav Eriksen, fifty-two, employed as a night watchman at the Slemdalsveien branch of the bank, was on duty alone, and by eleven o'clock had completed his rounds. He was preparing his night meal when he heard the front doorbell ring. It was then 11:07 P.M. The situation since the Germans came to take over was confused as regards banks, for measures about the control of assets and currency were in hand, but Eriksen's duties were clear. He had to protect the bank.

Eriksen thought it might be the police, who were taking special measures at that time in Oslo to guard the banks from looting or Resistance sabotage. He strapped on his

* As I later was given a carbon copy of this Resistance report, I know just what he read.

pistol and took his light and opened the door. The street was blacked-out and empty except for a German car. He had no doubt about the car being German. It was painted in *Wehrmacht* camouflage—a registered civilian car but now carrying an Army number.

Two men in uniform were in the car and the two German officers at the door. That is all Eriksen had time to notice, for the taller of the two German officers pushed roughly into the bank and the other followed close behind, closing the bank doors after him.

The first German drew his automatic when he saw the watchman's pistol. "Put that away!" he said in German. "You had a light showing and we are going to investigate this bank."

The watchman replied, "You Germans have no right in this bank."

At that the first German struck him a violent blow with the butt of his automatic pistol. This blow did not strike him unconscious, but as he fell the other German kicked him in the stomach, and as he collapsed struck him in the temple with the heel of his boot.

Eriksen had a fractured skull, and though he never entirely recovered, he survived and was able to give the above description of events that night.

Nothing more is known of the two men, except, by inference, that they were expert demolition engineers. The trail ends here, for at that time there were hundreds of such Germans in Oslo. The height of the taller German officer and the fact that he wore the general staff stripe on his breeches, and that the other also wore top boots—these are the only clues to their identity. The two must have been

high-ranking officers to have used a staff car without fear
of being stopped and questioned.

During the night of April 12–13 the strong-room doors
were blown off in the vaults of the bank at Slemdalsveien
and bullion to the value of over one million pounds sterling
carried away. No clues were left and no trace of this twenty
million kroner worth of gold, some of it in gold bar but
mostly in coins, has ever been found.

High-ranking German officers are thought to have been
concerned in the raid because (a) of the night watchman's
evidence, and (b) only high-ranking occupation authorities
knew of the presence of the gold in this branch of the bank,
this having been the subject of some informal talks that
had taken place between the directors of the bank, the
Quislings, and the German Command only the day before.

That was the gist of what Nils read out to me, and when
he had finished he replaced the document in his portfolio.
"Our chaps have kept their eyes open for that gold though,"
he told me. "The Resistance has been looking for it ever
since it disappeared. That amount cannot be moved about
without people getting to know, so our fellows watched
out. I think that was how they got on to Goerdler—or your
friend Jan, if you prefer it. They just waited until someone showed his hand. Goerdler did. That was what uncov-
ered him."

I began to realize what this meant now. "You mean
there was twenty million kroner worth of gold in the
Leonora? That Jan was one of those men who beat up the
night watchman at the bank?"

"Men will do strange things for gold."

"Twenty million kroner!"

"Our people," Nils said, "are very interested in your description of those heavy boxes with the stenciled lettering. They may be the original bullion boxes. They sound like it. But your friend Jan probably only had *his* share on the *Leonora*. The rest is still hidden away—who knows where?"

"How much was there on the *Leonora*, Nils?"

"Three boxes—about four million kroner worth. Two hundred thousand pounds. A nice little sum. They traced the man who moved it for him down to Maritim. He spoke under persuasion; he did not know where it went."

"To the bottom of the fjord," I said.

"It will be a nice little salvage job for someone, someday, perhaps. If you only knew where she went down . . . if she did go down."

I was thinking to myself: Jan was a Nazi informer. "I don't believe it," I said. "Jan is no Nazi. It's impossible."

"His job was to get information, not to denounce people. He kept you rolling. You might have told him anything in time."

"I told him nothing. And Jan was no informer."

"Three million dollars is a lot of money," Nils answered.

After a moment I said, "Nils, it is time to go to the hospital. Don't *you* go and get mixed up in this gold business. Let them fight it out. Let them have it—if they can find it."

"Yes," Nils answered. "Let's get along to Kirsti."

19

THE STRONGBOX

ON THE way to the Ullevaal Hospital Nils was strangely silent. I did not realize that he had had scarcely any sleep for nearly a week, and now that I had turned up again the news I brought was hardly of a sort to allow him peace of mind. We walked up the steps and went in the normal way to the waiting room—that sinister place where I had waited for Fru Hirschfeldt—while they telephoned to the ward. Then a man came in and, calling my name, said we might go up.

Hjoerdis was in the corridor waiting for me, and took us into the ward. "She's awake and normal," she said. "The temperature is down."

Kirsti was in a cot by the window, her straw-colored hair on the pillow about her face, and at first she did not see me. Then her eyes lit up and I moved close to kiss her. I could feel her cling to me.

"Where have you been, Mummy?" she asked me.

She looked very ill to me and my heart went out to her.

"In the mountains," I told her. "And I've got some butter *and* a ham."

"I've been waiting for you to come to me."

"I only just got back and Nils told me you were ill. So I came at once."

"Nils has been coming to see me," Kirsti said. "He brought me flowers." Her eyes turned to a cyclamen in a pot by the bed. "I think he stole it."

Nils was waiting by the door, talking with Hjoerdis. We both turned to look at him.

As it happened, Nils *had* stolen the cyclamen. There were practically no flowers to be had in Oslo, so Nils had "lifted" the cyclamen from the kitchen of a large house belonging to a Quisling councillor whose refrigerator he had been in the process of servicing when he heard of Kirsti's arrival at the hospital. Nils returned to the kitchen next morning and liberated the cyclamen. He had also, I found out later, brought her a pile of American comics, obtained heaven only knows where and how; these were much more popular with Kirsti than the children's books I brought in for her.

"You must hurry and get well," I told her. "I'm coming every day to see you—"

"No more for today," Hjoerdis said.

I had a talk with the doctor before I left. He could give me no reassurance. At that stage they were in the dark and were keeping her under observation on account of her temperature variations. Kirsti had most of the symptoms of polio, including persistent high temperature, but no crisis had developed yet.

After Nils left me I went back to bed and slept right

through until the next morning. It was in the afternoon of that following day that I went with two of our people to see if we could get hold of the contents—if any—of the box in the strong room at the Aker Sparebank. Nils arrived at the apartment, bringing with him a distinguished member of our group whom I must call Schultz. He was a lawyer and a member of parliament and formerly very influential. Schultz's wife was the bosom friend of an Englishwoman, Sonia Evensen, also married to a Norwegian, whom I knew very well—born in the same town as I was, although we had never met before we came together in Oslo.

Nils waited outside the bank, to be on hand if there was trouble. *Advokat* Schultz and I entered and walked up to the counter. Nils had said that when Jan was missed, the Gestapo would naturally make inquiries. It was possible that there would be some record of his strongbox. If so, they might keep watch. It was for this reason, among others, that our group wanted us to make an attempt to examine the box as quickly as possible.

"It is likely," Nils told me—he could always think of something to comfort you—"that a man who takes the precaution to keep a strongbox in a Norwegian bank also takes the trouble to keep the fact that he has it from becoming known. Especially in official quarters."

I did not like the idea that there might be someone waiting at the bank to see who would walk in and try to claim the box, and I said so at the time.

"But you knew him," Nils answered. "He was your personal friend over a long period. It might have been a box you shared. You have a first-class excuse if you are arrested. You are the best one for the job."

It was another of those things over which I had nothing
to worry! In any event, I had agreed to go along, so here I
was, just before closing time, walking up bold as brass to
the young man in glasses behind the counter. And my
"lawyer" was with me, just behind.

"I want to open a strongbox in your vaults," I said. And
at that moment it seemed to me all noise in the bank suddenly ceased and my voice rang out for all to hear.

"Your name, Madame?"

Mr. Schultz stepped forward and gave my correct name
and address, as we had arranged, for if there was going to
be trouble small lies would not help us, whereas the truth
would tend to support the claim that I was an innocent
friend—flimsy though that claim might prove.

The bank clerk left his place and went quickly into
the back offices. My heart missed a beat. If Mr. Schultz had
not been there I would have bolted. But the clerk came
back and asked us to enter a waiting room—the sort of
cubicle where you see the manager about your overdraft.
Mr. Schultz caught my eye and passed an unspoken warning; I gathered that he, too, had not quite liked the rapid
way the young clerk had disappeared as soon as my name
and the box had been mentioned. It certainly looked as if
he had been given previous orders and had acted on them.
We sat in silence for what seemed a very long time.

There was a ground-glass screen on my right, from the
neighborhood of which came a sustained clicking, probably
electric accounting machines at work, and from time to
time the outline of a girl's head and shoulders would move
across the screen on the far side. A clock on the mahogany
mantelpiece ticked like a time bomb.

When the door behind Mr. Schultz suddenly—and silently—opened, I jumped, but it was only an old man, bald as an egg, in a smart business suit. He had an air of authority. Just behind him came a porter, and the sight of the uniform really did make me nervous. The manager looked at me sharply but almost at once I saw that he was carrying a huge bunch of keys and I managed a smile.

"I thought you were going to attack me, with all that ironmongery," I said.

"No, Madame," the official told me gravely, "these are keys." In moments of tension the most idiotic remarks pass current.

Now that the manager had settled the business of keys not being lethal weapons, he opened up a beautifully bound ledger, and, adjusting his glasses, began to run one finger down an index column.

"Astrup . . . Ast . . . Ast-rup—I don't seem to trace any Astrup."

"The name would be Goffinger," I said.

He stopped his traveling finger as if frozen to the page, and looked up at me again very sharply. This is it, I thought. He's been waiting for that one word. He's pressing a secret alarm bell under the edge of the desk and bells are ringing at this very moment all over the bank. The Germans will come storming in and I shall be dragged out. In five minutes, I shall be at Victoria Terrasse after all, and they will be softening me up in the preliminary stages for questioning.

But the little bald man merely turned back to his ledger and began calmly to thumb through the pages again. "Goffing-er . . an unusual name. Goff . . . here we are. Joachim

Goffinger, Hotel Bristol. If you will let me have the password, Madame, on this slip?"

"This is my lawyer," I said. I had been ordered not to
leave anything in writing if I could help it. My "signature,"
if a receipt were demanded, was to be in handwriting as
much unlike my own as possible and not as I usually signed.
"He knows the password and I have no secrets from him.
It's—"

He closed the ledger protectively. "It must be written.
That is the regulation."

I wrote the word HELSINGFORS in block letters on the slip
and he accepted it coldly. He examined it, with suspicion
it seemed to me, then endorsed it with the date and his
initials, and slipped it away among his papers.

"I may wish to remove the box," I said. I had been told
to try this.

"That will be in order if you will pay any rent due and
sign a discharge."

"The key?" I held it up.

"You will need that to open the compartment in the
strong room. The bank carries no duplicates. Of course you
will surrender the key if you give up the tenancy of the
strong-room compartment."

He rose, bowed, and the porter opened the door. This
was all obviously routine and I felt greatly relieved. Evidently banks in occupied Oslo at that time did a brisk
business in strong-room boxes; the drill was all laid on. The
porter led the way down into the basement. Mr. Schultz
was not allowed in the strong room with us, so he waited
in the corridor outside, behind the first pair of grilled gates.

The vaults were chill and forbidding. They had an at-

mosphere in which the respectability of a bank struggled
without success to override the taint of a jail. Bare bulbs
spread fans of blinding white light about the tiles, and
shadows of bars streaked in a sinister way over the concrete
floor. The strong room was like a large hall, with a row of
double-sided desks down the center, each having a frosted
glass screen on either side for privacy.

I was thinking what queer sights this brilliantly lit
vault must witness on occasion, when a notion suddenly
came to me that the Germans only wanted to get hold of
the correct key before they arrested me. As soon as I pushed
the key in the locks, an alarm would ring and the sound of
their heavy boots would come as they rushed along the corridors. The devil! I thought. Alarms or not, I had to turn
the key now, so I turned it. The door swung open toward
me on a spring; inside was a metal box, and inside this box
was a writing case in morocco leather. No whistles blew;
the silence remained unbroken, and I breathed again.

I did not want to touch the box, and I hoped the porter
would lift it out for me, but he made no move. He just
stood there watching me.

"I may—take it?" I asked. It was quite small.

"But of course, Madame!"

I pulled the case out and shut the compartment. No one
seemed to mind. I turned around and walked toward the
steel grill, the porter following respectfully, pulling the
gates to after us and locking them securely with his huge
key. *Advokat* Schultz was there, impassive as ever, but I
noticed his eyes flick quickly to what I had under my arm.

The porter bowed us into the manager's office once
more, and there the little man was, waiting for us. I laid the

case on the table and with it the key to the compartment.
Mr. Schultz paid some money and got a receipt. I signed in
a disguised handwriting an official discharge, and before I
had time to realize it we were walking down the street outside the bank, safe and free, *with Jan's case firmly held
under my arm!*

We walked in silence, as arranged, in the direction of
Frogner, and so came to the stopping place where you wait
for the streetcars. We stood there in the queue.

It was at this exact spot that I had had a bad time some
months before, and so of course I began thinking how dangerous things have a habit of happening to you at certain
places, almost as if it were possible to have such things as
bad-luck spots. Kirsti and I had stopped here one night
when we had been out black-marketeering together. I had
managed to exchange some of my diminishing wardrobe
of warm clothing for a God-sent haul of nearly sixteen
pounds of stewing beef! Such traffic was dealt with very
severely. You could get as much as seven years' imprison-
ment if you were caught, and the black-market operator
himself could be executed. So one had to be very discreet
and cautious. Kirsti and I carried our precious load between us to the car stop. The meat was wrapped in Fritt
Folk newspapers, and I was in a hurry to get home because
it was not very secure. Our Quisling police as well as the
patrolling Germans had a habit of looking twice at suspicious parcels.

All went well until we got to the queue at the car stop.
A group of German soldiers with an officer stood on the
pavement by the square—a street patrol. An elderly Norwegian policeman was lounging nearby. The queue seemed

to be full of disagreeable and suspicious citizens, and our car, of course, was simply ages coming.

Kirsti's hand nudged me. I thought she was tired, or wished to complain about something, so at first I disregarded it. But then she nudged me urgently, and when I turned I saw her frightened eyes goggling up at me. Her fright made her speak in English, and to this day I can hear her voice ringing out clear as a bell over the crowded pavement.

"Mummy," she said, "there's blood coming all over the outside of the meat parcel."

I should think twenty people must have turned to stare, including some of the Germans, but apparently no one understood English. I opened my coat and thrust the parcel under it and prayed just about as hard as I have ever prayed for the car to arrive—which it did, fortunately almost at once. Half of Oslo seemed to be scowling at me as I climbed aboard.

Now, months later, at the same spot with Mr. Schultz, I was thinking: Something will happen here again. It is bound to, for I haven't been here since and wiped off the bad luck. This is where they come running out of the bank after us. . . .

I broke the rule of silence and said to Mr. Schultz, "I wish we could take a taxi from here."

I could see that that surprised him. He looked cautiously around and found nothing. "Don't panic!" he whispered back. "Everything went fine. And here's Pansy. . . ."

I saw out of the corner of my eye that Nils had joined the queue farther down. I stood my ground, trying to think of other things, but until the car came along all I could think of was the parcel of meat with the blood soaking through.

Nils broke the lock and the case when we got back to my flat. Lying on top of the contents was an envelope addressed to me. "Read it, my dear," Mr. Schultz said. After a moment Nils added, "What are you waiting for?"

Neither of them knew that Jan had asked me to marry him. I certainly did not want to open the letter in front of anyone. I took the envelope to my desk in the window and tore open the flap.

Jan began by saying that since I was reading this note something must have happened to him, and that he wished me to have the contents of the case, which he prized. The letter was dated more than a year before, at a time when I imagined I had on my hands nothing more than a rather nice person, with exquisite manners, who wanted to improve his English. To think that even then he was writing letters like this to me was a revelation.

There were three pages to this letter—I have them still —and in these pages Jan said a lot of foolish things, but they touched me nevertheless very much. I thought that, whatever he might or might not have done, he was a very brave man. I thought of him walking down the jetty with his foot trailing. . . .

"Well?" Nils asked at length.

"He says the box belongs—belongs to me."

"Finish the job. Go through it."

"You do it," I said.

I heard Nils tipping the case on the polished parquet floor and the sound was heavy. "Quite a bit of gold here!" I heard Nils exclaim.

There was nearly six hundred pounds' worth of gold, mostly in German pieces and English sovereigns. An expensive old-fashioned gold hunter watch with Jan's father's name engraved in the back and some men's jewelry were tucked away among the papers. In a sentimental German way there was even a ribbon-tied lock of his mother's hair and a single baby shoe. Mr. Schultz pounced on a birth certificate. It was in the name of Johan Joachim Albrecht Goerdler.

"That's all we shall want," Mr. Schultz said at length, when they had examined everything.

"What about all this?" I asked them.

"It's yours. But I wouldn't advertise it. There are people who would cut your throat for half that amount of gold. Hide it away." Mr. Schultz turned to Nils. "Right?"

"You're right," Nils said briefly. "This hasn't helped us much—" He put a hand on mine. "I'm sorry, Helen," he said in a soft voice.

"It doesn't matter," I told him. "It doesn't make any difference, does it?"

Nils shook his head. Then the two of them carefully placed the papers they wanted in a large envelope and left me. After a while I pulled myself together. I did not want so much gold lying about the place, so I put it all in my sponge bag and hid it with the rest of my hoard in the bathroom under the floor boards. I repacked the writing case and put it away with my other things. I have it to this day.

20

ASSIGNMENT: SPYING
ON FRIENDS

IN THE WEEKS that followed I developed a routine which took me to the hospital each day. I also spent a lot of time out in the country buying extra food for Kirsti. I was no longer distributing the newsheet. I had the idea I was not so welcomed at the shop at Bogstadveien, and since I no longer called there I got no extra food. There would be days when Kirsti could not recognize anyone, tossing and turning in delirium, followed by days when she appeared almost normal—days in which she rapidly regained her strength. At that time a wave of polio swept Oslo and hundreds died—many of them children. But Kirsti struggled on.

Of course Kirsti's illness overshadowed everything. I scarcely thought about anything else, but looking back now, I can see that I must have realized that my relations with the rest of our group were changed. I think there was a question mark in the background where I was concerned. In conditions such as prevailed in Oslo in those days of the occupation, suspicion was inevitable.

You had to be suspicious of everything and of everyone. Your life so often depended on it. If you have to give great trust to your fellowmen it follows that you have to give great suspicion, too. I do not blame the rest of our group. However innocently, I *had* been a close friend of Goerdler, and there was now a slight reserve when they dealt with me.

The Germans naturally had to be discreet. With an important man like Jan, inquiries would have to pass through channels. They would have to wait to be examined in high places, but always those inquiries would go on. Important people would want to know in the end what had happened to him, and this would mean high-power investigation that had to produce results, or else. Without a doubt the Gestapo would in time dig into every fact they could scrape up about Jan. Sooner or later some reference to me would turn up, and the inquiry would move in my direction. This was something both Nils and I underestimated.

Nils was always my champion. He never said much but he did a good deal, and I am sure that whenever the need arose he would point out the helpful work I had done on one or two occasions—particularly with regard to Fru Hirschfeldt and her little girl. I believe now that Nils was behind the last job I had to do for the Resistance in Oslo. I believe he wanted to reestablish me among my friends and remove the question mark forever. Otherwise he would never have allowed me to take the risk. But before this, early in the summer, the case of the Evensens came up.

Kirsti had been let out of the hospital to live once more with me at home. She was convalescing and required good feeding. The temperature symptoms had disappeared, but she was by no means strong. Her limbs and movements were unaffected. The doctors at the hospital never were sure what was wrong with her. No crisis ever developed, but she grew very weak before she began finally to mend. I had lived for weeks expecting the telephone to ring with the news that was haunting me, but it never did. Kirsti recovered, and she came home to me. I could have wept from sheer relief.

I had often stayed with Sonia Evensen at her house at Vettakollen in Oslo. Her husband had been a member of parliament and they had a country place up in the mountains, where he owned hundreds of miles of forest. They also had a luxurious cabin cruiser which they kept in Bestumkilen; before the war I made several trips with them in their boat. Sonia and I had never met in Bath, where we were brought up, but we had the town and our common school to draw us together. I knew the house at Vettakollen well, and it was because I knew the house and had stayed there that I was assigned to this job. And it was because dear old Nils knew the kitchens—Nils and his refrigerators! —that he went along, too. I think this was the first step in my rehabilitation.

Having an important man like Anders Evensen on our side was a great help to the movement. From the start he had been a member of the underground. His official position made it difficult for him to work openly among us, and he was—so Nils informed me—always an undercover man, right from the beginning. He was invaluable because of the contact his position gave him with the Nazi bosses. That was the setup when a secret raid was made by Resistance leaders on his offices in town, not by our group, but by another. There was reason to suspect that someone had betrayed plans, and this group had lost four men—executed. They could only have been caught by a leakage of information at a vital point, possibly at Evensen's level.

Nothing definite was found at Evensen's offices, and he never knew the raid had been made. But very high up in the organization it was decided to explore a little farther. Nils was to take me along to have a quiet look over the Evensens' house while they were away.

I did not like the idea at all. To steal into anyone's house and burgle it was bad enough, but to sneak into the house of a friend—?

I had always liked Anders—a big, blond man with a very loud voice and a hearty sense of humor. He was fond of shooting and fishing and yachting—you could only picture him against an outdoor life. I could not see him as one who would send or let four countrymen go to their death, but Nils said this was a job that had to be done, and furthermore that if nothing were found in the house we would be doing Sonia and Anders a good turn.

Rich men are subject to temptations the ordinary man in the street can never know. Nils and others seemed to think they had good cause to be uneasy about Anders. I tried to convince myself that that was reason enough for me, but I could not bring myself to like the job; instinctively I was against it.

The opening move was for me to find out Sonia's movements; so I telephoned her, as ordered, gossiped for a while, and got myself invited out to the big house for tea. I went round to see Nils the next day, and he said he would come out with me to scout around, since we would have to find some place nearby to lie up, waiting for nightfall, on the day we planned to break in.

The Evensens' house lay back from the road in its own grounds. Nearest to the roadway, at the gates of the drive, were the stables and garages. Up until the war some of the outdoor servants had lived over the garages, but they had long since departed, and the horses were gone. I told Nils about this, and he left me at the gates to look around the buildings, while I walked on up the drive.

Sonia must have seen me, for she came out on the porch to welcome me. She seemed careworn and tired—no doubt the strain showed in us all—but she was genuinely glad to see me again. She asked me if I had any plans about getting back to England on the "Shetland Bus."* I told her I had no plans. I told her about Kirsti. . . . We had a lot to talk about.

Anders came in later, and, as usual, he adopted a brotherly, teasing way with me. But I could tell he was worried. Sonia said he had little to do at his business. The restrictions made things practically impossible. I asked questions about the servants and their movements, as I had been ordered, and all the time I felt like a sneak thief. I wondered what Anders would think if he knew what was going on in my mind . . . that I was going to creep into his house later and rout around in his private affairs. I thought: If he has nothing to conceal, he would approve. If he is hiding something, it is my duty to uncover it. The idea should have helped, but it didn't.

* As they called it in Norway—the small boats that in the fine summer weather sneaked out in dozens every week from northern ports and made the Shetland Islands.

Anders was a peculiar sort of man. He had a one-track mind on the subject of sports. He simply could not understand how anyone like me had managed to achieve mature years without taking up bicycle riding as a sport. I have never liked riding a bicycle. I hate lawn tennis and have never held a racket. I would sooner be kicked by wild horses than play the game of hockey (much the same thing in the end). I loathe shooting things. All this was just incomprehensible to Anders. I am sure that if it were not for the lucky accident of my being able to swim, and to leave him standing on skis, he would have avoided me long since as a freak of nature.

I found out that the Evensens were leaving that week end as usual for Lillehammer, in the mountains. Anders had an allowance of gasoline for his business, and was going by car. This time they were also taking the old married couple who were now the only servants they had. It might have been arranged especially to suit Nils and his friends.

After I left I had not gone far on the road to the station before Nils caught up with me. He told me that he had decided we should hide in some old greenhouses on an adjoining estate which were both nearer the Evensens' house and farther from the road than the stables. Then I made my own report. "I'm sure he has done nothing wrong," I said.

"Fine!" Nils agreed. "Then your conscience can be quite easy."

"That's all very well, but they are not your friends."

"If you like," Nils said, "since you like worrying about things so much, you can think that the sort of humdrum job we are doing now protects the lives of the men who have to do the really dangerous jobs later. If it wasn't for the little people uncomplainingly doing the little jobs, the movement wouldn't last a week."

On the following Saturday afternoon Nils and I went out again to Vettakollen, allowing plenty of time for him to look around before we took up our hiding place to wait for darkness. I wore an old pair of skiing slacks and a raincoat. I had light shoes on, and carried a bag—almost every woman in those days carried a bag, for all the time one looked for food. The lane in which the Evensens lived was deserted, but as we approached the gates we saw a policeman on a bicycle talking to another on the curb. We walked past them and continued along for a while. When we came back they were gone; not a soul was in sight.

We entered the grounds and Nils made me walk up to the front door and ring the bell—to make sure the house was empty, in case they had changed their plans. If anyone had answered I could easily have thought up something to say, but no one answered. With Nils at my heels, I walked round the lawn in front of the French windows, through the oak door in the garden wall, across the kitchen into the vegetable garden, and down the path toward the hard tennis courts. The greenhouses Nils had picked were just the other side of the yew hedge here, and we made our way through.

Nils had a thermos and some sandwiches, but we kept these refreshments for later. We sat for hours, in a deserted garden, out of sight, in the moldy atmosphere distinctive of all greenhouses. I had never realized before what a clatter birds can make in a silent garden merely by flying about. Blackbirds sound like police rattles after a while.

Apart from the birds, nothing came our way—not even a cat—and by the time it began to grow dark I was almost paralyzed with cramp and boredom.

Nils got up and took out his flashlight. "Leave everything here," he said. "We'll collect it later. Ready?"

21

STRANGERS IN THE HOUSE

THE SUN had set. Although there was some light left in the sky, the garden was wrapped in an impenetrable grayness. The trees and the bushes and the darker shapes of the buildings had a sinister air. A moment ago it was all friendly, and I was bored; now a tingle ran up my spine. The place was hostile. I would gladly have gone back to the greenhouse.

Nils pressed on. "Keep away from the flowerbeds," he warned, and began to make a tour of the old house, trying the windows. He wanted to avoid leaving prints behind to let anyone know we had been on the prowl, and he was particularly anxious to not have garden soil on our shoes when we got inside the place. When he whispered to me I answered by nodding—I was not too sure of my voice. I was thinking: What if they've come back? What if they're at home now?

We did not have far to prowl, for Nils found a suitable pantry window almost at once. He managed to slip the catch, then pulled on his gloves and climbed up. Before he swung his legs inside he carefully wiped the soles of his shoes with a rag he had brought along with him for the purpose. Then he disappeared, and for a long time I waited alone outside, feeling terribly conspicuous. It was eerie out here in the garden, so quiet and still; I wished he would hurry. My eyes were fixed on the sill over which he had climbed, waiting for him to reappear and pull me up, and so I did not hear him open the kitchen door. "Psst!" he hissed at me, and I almost jumped out of my skin. I moved quickly to where he stood. After I had wiped my shoes on the mat, he lifted each foot separately and wiped the shoe with his rag.

"Take the flashlight," Nils said, "and show me around the living rooms. Keep the light from the windows, in case the blackout is not drawn." Shining a small circle of light on the floor before me, I tiptoed out of the kitchens and into the hall. I was thinking: We're in and we're doing the job. I tried vainly to make it prosaic.

I never knew just what Nils had orders to look for among Anders's papers and among his clothes. An identity card was one of the things, because Nils told me to keep an eye out for anything that looked like that. Any picture or snapshot of a young girl who was *not* one of the family was another. We found neither. But Nils was looking for other things.

The main hall had a huge fireplace and a staircase with a gallery. Anders's study was next to the porch on the east, while to the west was a long drawing room. The place looked bigger still in the beam of the flashlight. Nils crossed into the study, and took the light from me while he went through the drawers of the desk. I could not help thinking he was making too much noise. I prayed he would hurry, but nothing ever rattled Nils. He always took his time. He made a thorough search, and often there were agonizing halts while he stood perfectly still and read some paper that interested him. The house was full of creaks and sighs; a hundred times I imagined I heard someone creeping up on us. But at last my partner was satisfied. We went quickly through the rest of the rooms on the ground floor.

"Has he a wall safe?" Nils asked me. I told him that as far as I knew there wasn't one.

"I'm only interested now in his bedroom, or his dressing room," Nils said. "Take me up there."

I crept up the stairs, hugging the paneled wall. What kept me pinned to the wall was the thought: If Sonia suddenly appeared and started to come down the stairs!

The circle of light went on step by step before me, and the sound of Nils's heavy tread followed behind. On the landing my foot slipped on the polished wood and I almost fell.

"Take it easy," Nils growled. "If you break your neck I don't know what I shall do with you."

"In that case I wouldn't have to worry," I told him.

We continued a few feet. "This is Mrs. Evensen's bedroom," I said. "His is beyond, and there's a dressing room beyond that."

"Where does he keep his clothes?"

"In his dressing room. There's a built-in wardrobe, but I think there's another in the bedroom itself. Nils—please hurry!"

"Take it easy," he repeated.

A trace of tobacco smoke lingered in Anders's bedroom;

in the dressing room was the smell of tweeds and shoe pol-
ish. Nils took the light from me again and disappeared into
the wardrobe.

"Is there anything you want me to look for?" I asked
him.

"Never mind," he said shortly.

He seemed to be examining the cuffs of all the jackets
he could find. In the end he took a golf jacket—the type
of garment with a zip fastener up the front and a short
waist—and stuffed it in his coat pocket. Then he began
a scrutiny of the shoes and boots in the cupboard. One pair
of shoes kept him some time—he examined every inch of
them. Then he said he would have to take these along, too.
He wrapped the shoes in the golf jacket and buckled a belt
around the parcel.

"Time's getting on," he said—as if no one had noticed
the fact! "We'll have to pull out soon."

It could not have been soon enough for me. "Have you
found anything, Nils?" I asked.

"Maybe something with these shoes. We have a photograph of an impression made by the man we're after."

"And the jacket?"

"Perhaps. Does he ever wear a golf jacket without playing golf?"

"Sometimes. Yes, I've seen him wearing one about the
house."

"Well, I guess we can go."

We were coming down the staircase into the hall, Nils
with the flashlight and I close behind him, when we heard
the front door open in the darkness ahead.

In the split second when whoever it was turned to close

the door behind him, Nils flicked off his light. I was transfixed. I hadn't really expected anything to happen. Fortunately Nils realized at once that the next move for anyone
would be to switch on lights, so he dragged me back into
the alcove on the half landing, where there was a long window seat and heavy curtains—and not a moment too soon.
The light in the hall seemed to come on at once. I saw that
it was Anders.

He went into the dining room. We heard him at a cupboard, then came the clink of a glass. I heard the splash of
a siphon and could imagine what he was doing next. I
wanted to bolt, to do anything except stand still where I
was, but there was Nils's restraining hand on my arm. "He
won't know anyone's here," came the whisper. "I must see
what he's come back for."

"I've got to get out!"

"All in good time! Don't lose your head."

I heard Anders's step again, as he left the dining room
to cross quickly into his study. The lights came on there,
and, then for a long time—it seemed to me—nothing further happened. I reflected that it was rather odd anyone
should change his plans and come home just to drink a
whisky and soda in his study.

Nils put his lips close to my ear. "Stay here and don't
make a noise—I'm going down to see what he's up to."

"No, no, Nils!" I begged. "Don't leave me here alone!"

"Want to come with me?"

I shook my head. He left me, treading silently as an
Indian down the stairs, and in spite of myself I had to
watch him disappear around the corner. Then I shut my
eyes. This was tempting providence too far.

When at last I plucked up enough courage to open my eyes, I could see Nils with his face glued to the crack of the door hinge. The minutes seemed to stretch on. From time to time something in the house would creak, or groan, or sigh like a woman. Apart from this there was no sound to break the tension.

"Nils! Nils!" I was calling out to myself. "Come back and let's go! Nils!" To be so obstinate!

Suddenly I saw Nils slip aside and dive into the darkness of the porch. Anders came heavily out of his study, and to my horror made straight for the stairs.

I watched him come, nearer and nearer. I couldn't have done a thing to save my life. It seemed too obvious that he would see me there shaking behind the curtain, and drag me out. Then what would I do? What would I say?

Anders came within three feet of me and passed on to his bedroom.

. No sign of Nils.

I wondered if he had made himself scarce, but I knew, on second thought, he would never do a thing like that. Did he expect me to race down the stairs, fly across the hall, and dive out into the night? The plan had an enormous attraction, but I stayed where he had told me to. In moments of crisis, stay put.

After a while I saw Nils's head emerge around the corner of the porch. He looked up toward me and made a face of inquiry. I realized he could not see what I could, so I signaled that Anders had gone into the bedroom, pointing with my arm. Instead of beckoning me down, Nils came up the stairs with a rush to join me behind the curtain.

"He's got pretty nearly every light in the place on.

Lucky there's blackout curtains or someone might come in to see what's going on here."

"Nils," I besought him. "Let's *go!* You've got all you want."

"I want to see what his next move is," Nils said. "Be patient for just a little while longer. You're doing well." I didn't care how I was doing. I had a conviction that we had stayed too late. The house remained quiet as we waited, except for the creaking and groaning that went on without cease, and the presentiment grew on me: Something was going to happen, and it was going to happen soon.

It happened. The front door in the dimly lit hall below began to open. Although I was not looking in that direction, I became aware of it at once. I jogged my intent companion and pointed dumbly. Nils, throwing an irritated glance over his shoulder, saw me and shot his eyes down the stair. I felt him tense up like a coiled spring.

Anders, we knew, was still in his room. *This could not be he.* I remember thinking that of all nights open to me I would have to go and pick this one when there was probably going to be a double murder. Nils was right. Something must be in the air if Anders had gone to the precaution of covering up his tracks—stealing out of Oslo and slipping back in again in the dead of the night. What was going on? Was this newcomer following Anders?

The door opened fully but for a while we saw no one. Then when the opening of the door had drawn no countermove from inside, a face appeared. A woman came in and looked quickly around, then made a sign to someone waiting outside. Whereupon the strangest collection of human beings I had seen for a long time trooped obediently in.

The woman leader carefully closed the door, bolted it, and herded the group without a sound into the study on the left. Nils and I exchanged startled looks.

There were in all eight persons in the party. All were women except one very old man whose head (though it was a warm night) was swathed in an enormous woolen scarf, and a boy of about fourteen in a skiing suit. Two of the women had babies in their arms, and the lot of them, the old man included, had rucksacks and sticks. Several carried other bundles. But before we had time to ponder the sight, the leader came back into the hall and, seeing the lights upstairs, climbed up, past our curtain, and disappeared along the landing. I saw her face quite clearly.

"Nils," I whispered, "that's Irma Jensen from the place where they hand out the sheets in Sumsgate; I know her face quite well. She helps to work the *roneo* and she has handed me my bundle dozens of times. She's one of us, Nils."

"There's one thing about this job that sticks out a mile," Nils replied. "We don't know anything, though what's going on here concerns us pretty closely right now. The Germans probably know all about it. The Quislings, of course, are keeping an eye on it. The police have made a careful note about it—but us? Oh no! We never know what the rest of the Joessings are up to. This little lot is due to make a trip over the mountains, wouldn't you think?"

"Then—Anders came back for this? His visit to Lillehammer was only a blind?"

"There's no reason why he shouldn't take them up there to start them off. Hand them over to someone else. You're sure about the girl?"

"I couldn't make a mistake," I hesitated. "Nils—do you think we ought to step out and let them know we're here?"

"Not on your life! But we might as well go now. This is a new angle and I'm sure our group can't know about it. These folks are certainly here to go over the border, and that can only mean us. . . . I'll go first," he ordered. "You wait until you are sure no one has noticed me getting out, then follow as quickly as you can. Once you have started don't stop for anything—if all hell breaks loose—keep straight on. You always stand a much better chance of getting away if you make use of those first few seconds while the other side is gathering its wits."

"All right," I said. As long as we were going, I would have agreed to anything.

Nils slipped out and down the stairs. He was gone in a flash and I heard no sound at all. I forced myself to wait; the impulse to start running as soon as Nils did was very strong. At length I decided it was time for me to have a try.

I raced down the stairs. As I reached my shadows by the green baize doors leading to the kitchen someone at the door of the study called out softly, "Irma!" I did not even look back. As Nils had instructed, I kept right on. My feet were flying when I reached the kitchen, but there I quickly came to a halt. One of the women was at the sink. How she had got there without our seeing her pass down the hall, I cannot imagine. The shock was sharp, and it was I who had to gather my wits. I stood and gaped.

As the woman turned to see who had come, I nodded dumbly. After a pause, she smiled. Suddenly I realized she thought I was merely someone about the house—I should have known that would be the natural reaction. At once I said, *"Good aften."*

"Good aften," she replied, and turned back to her washing.

I slipped by into the scullery. The door was unlatched, and I crept quietly out into the pitch-blackness of the night. I was never so thankful in my life to be out of any place. Someone said *Psst!* and Nils's hand came out of the darkness to touch my elbow and guide me. He led the way unconcernedly back to the greenhouses, and there made a place for me with a rug. Shading the flashlight, he began to pour out hot coffee.

"Didn't you see a woman in the kitchen at the sink?" I demanded.

He nodded. "Washing a baby's bottle. Sandwich?"

"But what did she *say* when you walked in on her?"

"She said *'Good natt.'* What did you expect her to say? 'Help! Burglars'? The last thing she expected to see was a burglar."

I drank the hot coffee gratefully and shared the sandwiches. They were made of veal, so I knew that Nils had been doing a little more liberating on my behalf. One of the advantages of working in rich men's kitchens—and in the refrigerator at that—is that you have access to things denied to the less fortunately placed. Privately I think Nils used to do very well out of his work.

While I ate I reflected: Nils may be as casual as he likes about the woman at the sink, but as of any moment she is liable to drop a remark that will be dynamite in that house.

Later Nils wrapped the rug around my knees, then went off to sleep crouched as he was, his head on his knees.

I could not, so I sat and shivered for the brief remainder of the night. Sometime later I heard a car move off, which I took to be Anders and his party on the move.

When it was light enough to see, I stole out and liberated a bagful of vegetables from the garden for myself and Kirsti. Then I waked Nils. I felt like a brute, he was so evidently worn out, but he woke cheerful as ever and we set off down the drive of the Evensens' house as if we owned the place. I did not tell Nils about the bag of vegetables— it would have been just like him to make me empty it in the bushes in case we were stopped and questioned. However, there was no difficulty. We caught a workman's early-morning train at the station and were back in my apartment before seven o'clock. I went to bed, but Nils was off on his day's work among refrigerators.

22

A CALL FOR PANSY

A FEW DAYS before Nils and I set out to investigate Anders Evensen, an incident occurred which caused some uneasiness among our people. A woman called one afternoon on the telephone asking for *"Pansy."* She was given a guarded answer, and she then identified herself as an employee at the cigarette counter of a leading hotel which I will call the Bristol. She was told she would be called back, and she gave us a number at which to reach her. Nothing more passed at this first contact, but the group did not like the incident.

Our telephone number was a special one, as far as I know unique in our sort of work. Only a selected few knew it, and it was only used in urgent cases, or when it was passed on to someone outside our immediate circle who wanted to make contact and had no other means of reaching us. Our meeting places changed a good deal, but the number always remained—for emergency.

Many of the people who worked at the telephone exchange were reliable, and two men who generally worked at night were active Joessings, though not in our group. Our telephone number was in fact no number at all. It was what is called a "spare" at the automatic exchange, and the operator there could pick up the call and answer it. Contacts we wanted could then be passed on to the ordinary telephone at Frognerveien, while those it seemed best to avoid could be stopped. The number could never be traced to anyone, anywhere.

Anders Dahl, the chemist—the man who was the keen miniature-camera user—called this girl's number from his shop, without disclosing himself.

She turned out to be a beautiful blonde named Ingrid Quist, who worked, as she said, at the cigarette counter. The routine check we employed proved she was the right person; by arrangement Nils called the number she had given, and Dahl, keeping watch, saw her answer the phone. He saw her talking to Nils, overheard part of the conversation—so this *was* the girl who wanted to join us.

What the group still did not like was this girl's first questions. When she called our number she had been insistent on asking who was talking to her. No one who had been given our number genuinely would have done that. Subsequently Dahl found out without much trouble that the girl was a friend of several highly placed German officers. She was seen openly with them, and now she said she wished to be of some help to the organization. She explained that her position gave her special opportunities of reporting the movements of important Nazi bosses, which was true enough. She might well be genuine; people have changed their minds and come to their senses. But the men at Frognerveien did not like the look of this affair. Nils was sure the girl had been planted by the Gestapo to try and discover the identity of as many of the group as possible.

Up to the time of my wild night at the Evensens' house at Vettakollen, Ingrid Quist had spoken to only two of our people, and these of course she had no means of tracing. Now, Nils decided to make use of her.

The first I knew of all this was when Mr. Dahl took the opportunity, while I was in his shop buying some aspirin, to let me know that he and Nils were coming to see me that night. I knew what to do; after I had put Kirsti to bed, I went down to the basement, all innocent of what lay ahead.

I let Pettersen see me when I slipped down to the furnaces, so he would tell Nils when he arrived. As usual, the *vaktmester* would keep an eye on things, in case it became necessary for anyone to make a hurried exit.

I had not long to wait. Dahl came first, and when Nils joined us they got down to business. Nils said that there was a job to be done of the greatest importance to us all. Was I interested?

Nils looked at me steadily and quietly when he asked this question. It was as if he were saying, not for Dahl's benefit, "Here is the chance to settle the Goerdler matter for good." With a kind of sinking feeling I knew that what he had in mind was something more than sneaking into a house, or even the job with Fru Hirschfeldt.

There was a good reason for Nils to be so serious. This was a bad time for the underground movement in Norway. In the beginning the Germans had not expected much resistance—I think they were led astray because the Norwegians were so terribly unprepared to defend themselves— and so, when the movement developed, it was a surprise;

but by now they had begun to take countermeasures which were leveling a deadly toll of Resistance workers. In particular, at this time, they were helped by some bungle by British operatives dropped in the country which led to their getting hold of a secret radio and its mixed Norwegian-British crew intact.

The Germans, with the codes and passwords, carried on, and it was months before the War Office in London suspected anything was wrong. The Germans spoke twice a day with London at fixed hours, got all the secret messages—which alone practically broke up the organization of the underground—and arranged for drops to take place by parachute. These drops were awaited; of course, by the Germans, and time after time the RAF played into their hands.

The skill and daring of the agents who were dropped into Norway or sent over by fishing boats was beyond all praise, but from what I heard and saw there was a lot of stupidity and red tape among the officials back in London, which did not help matters at all. I say this as an Englishwoman; when it comes down to brass tacks there is no class so opinionated and hidebound as the British civil servant, and it is only when an Englishman breaks away from this tradition that he becomes one of the world's most dangerous fighting men—like the men who came to Norway during this period and later on.

So this was the situation lying behind my meeting with Nils and Anders Dahl. When he saw that I wasn't going to say no, Nils explained what had come up. An Englishman from Bristol, by the name of Frobisher, had been passed on to us by a reliable man at Bergen. The Bergen fisherman had the right to know our telephone number, and he acted correctly in passing it on to Frobisher, who had telephoned and eventually spoken with Nils. The group wanted this man checked, to see if he really was what he pretended to be. Bristol is near Bath, and there were several questions I could drop into any conversation innocently enough, to find out whether he really came from there.

"This man says he came in a Norwegian fishing boat called the *Aksel,*" Nils went on. "He says the boat was shot up by a German aircraft and sank, and that he got away as the only survivor. He eventually reached our man at Bergen, who passed him on to us."

"Naturally we made inquiries," Dahl told me. "We found that a Norwegian boat called the *Aksel* is based at a place called Lunna in the Shetlands, and that she *is* missing. Frobisher gave the skipper's name as Larsen. We have checked that too. Larsen is one of the skippers the British send out in these boats from the Shetlands. This man's story all tallies so far. We just want to make sure."

"You want me to meet him and ask questions about Bristol?" I asked.

"He wants—naturally enough—to contact us as quickly as possible and get our help. He lost everything when the *Aksel* sank. He could not make the contacts he was supposed to make. We can't check on that, of course, for he wouldn't tell us those anyway. Not if he's genuine—which we have no reason to doubt," Dahl said. "But remember: If the Germans have sunk the *Aksel,* they would know they sank her, wouldn't they? They would know where and how and when. They would probably know there had been an English agent aboard. An ideal situation for a plant."

"Don't let him scare you," said Nils. "We've checked up on this chap and so far there's nothing to be suspicious of. No one has seen him yet, but we are going to make a rendezvous—and you're going to keep it."

This was the classic way the Germans had of picking up Resistance men. From the rendezvous it was a short journey to Victoria Terrasse. A good deal of lurid writing has been done about the Germans and the means they had of extracting information, but the hard fact remains that torture *was* used as that means and it was almost invariably successful. The implications were far from pleasant to turn over in the mind. "Where?" I asked.

"We haven't fixed anything up yet, but Frobisher will call us this evening at nine o'clock to keep contact. We are going to set tomorrow at the National Teatret Station. "You'll go?" he asked, but already he knew my answer.

"I'll go. You will have to explain what I have to do."

"Just meet him where we say. Suggest going to a café or a movie—it's always the best to choose a crowded café or a movie. Then you just talk to him—ask him the right questions—and later leave. Tell him the next move will come when he telephones again. Then all you have to do is let me know whether you think he's all right, or not."

I did not really understand—it was just as well—that what happened after the first ten seconds was of secondary importance. Either tough-looking Germans in civilian clothes closed in on you from concealment as you exchanged recognition signals with the decoy, and it was all over, or no one appeared and the man would probably turn

out to be what he held himself to be—and safe. The first
ten seconds counted.

That night I had trouble in getting Billy back into his
cage. I let him fly around the room sometimes, and usually he would go back into his cage to put himself to bed;
but tonight he chose to be willful, and it was some time
before I trapped him. Then, when I finally did get to bed,
I lay awake.

I had seen the Gestapo pick up a man in the streets of
Oslo; the sudden swoop of big, basilisk-eyed Germans moving like automatons as they threw a Norwegian about as
if he were a sheep's carcass . . . the ghastly look in the little
man's eyes as they dragged him bleeding into the car . . .
these were things I couldn't forget. I was thinking, too, of
the *vaktmester* of the neighboring block of apartments who
had had his nails pulled out. But in the end I dozed off.
I knew about the danger but I did not feel it in my bones,
intimately. No one was likely to tear my nails out of my
fingers. I was just going to meet someone who was in trouble—an English boy from the RAF called Frobisher.

23

THE LAST JOB

THE PLAN called for me to be waiting in the Palm Court of the Bristol at eleven o'clock next morning, as smartly dressed as was then possible for me. This inevitably meant my gray squirrel coat, a little worn-looking now but still presentable. I was there on the minute, and Dahl joined me at once—he was already there waiting. He was the only one so far who had seen Ingrid Quist, and he now walked with me by the counter and bought a glossy German magazine. I watched the girl who handed him the magazine. She was really rather lovely in a typically Norwegian way, with genuine ash-blond hair, fine as silk, and sea-blue eyes.

When we were leaving the hotel Dahl said to me, "That's her. That's Ingrid. Remember her." I tucked her image away in my mind, though she was not a girl it would be easy to forget.

The meeting had been arranged with Frobisher for seven o'clock that evening at the National Teatret Station. This is a busy subway station in the center of Oslo which handles a lot of local traffic. At the entrance there is a long seat, decked in summer with masses of flowers, which faces the pavement, and this is a favorite meeting place in Oslo, especially for young men and women. Here at the time of the occupation you could always find Germans and Norwegian girls who did not mind associating with them. In fact, there were generally to be found at the National Teatret Station a few ladies who were looking for anyone who might be disposed to favor them. Not a pleasant spot for a woman to hang about in, but it was not quite so bad below the street level.

There were two means of access to the trains below: an entrance with a flight of stairs on one side of the bench and the flower boxes, and an exit on the other. Halfway down to the platform was a kind of ticket hall with magazine stands and telephone booths. Swinging doors gave access at several points to this hall. It is to the fact that the swinging doors were just where they happened to be that I perhaps owe my life.

I arrived at the National Teatret Station just before six-thirty, and went down to the ticket office to buy myself a ticket to hold in readiness against a search if the Germans or their Quisling servants suddenly sprang a control for any reason; also I had a good story prepared, giving a reason for my journey. I looked over the place just to make sure I remembered everything, picked my telephone booth, which was part of the plan, then went up the exit stairs and out to the pavement once more.

The bench was crowded as usual. It was a fine evening —one of those crisp clear Oslo days when the sun sparkles like glass and the clouds ride the sky like puffs of cotton

wool. The crowds coming and going was a safety factor,
Nils explained. Lots of things can happen in a crowd, without anyone noticing, and that was why they had chosen
this place. I still had nearly half an hour to kill, so I went
into a café nearby to pass the time and keep out of sight.

I took a seat at a table in the back of the café and ordered a pot of tea—herb tea, of course, which tasted of
bitter hay and was drunk without milk—and it was while I
was sipping this noxious stuff and thinking of what lay
ahead that one of those almost unbelievable coincidences
came along that can only occur in real life. No writer of
fiction would ever dare to use such material.

A young man came in off the street carrying two tennis
rackets. As soon as I saw them, a peculiar tingling sensation
moved up my spine to the nape of my neck.

Except for three people at a table by the door, we were
alone in the café. The newcomer chose a small table not
ten feet from where I sat. He was blond and fit, wearing a
pull-over such as Norwegian women knit for their menfolk,
gray flannel trousers and a gray soft hat. He looked like the
sort of man you expect to find in the RAF and he had a
clipped blond mustache. He put the rackets under the seat
of his chair, sat down, and looked at his wrist watch. Then
he gave me a casual look and his eyes passed on in search
of the waitress—who, since this was a young man, by some
chance happened to be immediately at hand.

I knew at once that this was the English boy I was to
meet. His appearance tallied from mustache to pull-over,
and my contact was to be carrying two tennis rackets, one
of which he would spin in his right hand from time to time
as he waited by the ticket windows. It was possible that two

blond men with mustaches might be carrying tennis rackets at seven o'clock at the National Teatret Station, but it was unlikely that there would be two men carrying two rackets each, and the identification became almost a certainty if one kept spinning one racket in his right hand.

I had lost interest in the tea. I remember thinking that Frobisher looked like a nice boy and that in spite of all the courageous things he had recently been through he seemed none the worse. My impulse was to catch his eye and say to him over the tables, "Can I get a ticket here for Roea?" I was the one, of course, who had to make the actual contact, and this was what I had to ask him as he stood by the ticket window. Frobisher had been told by our people to answer me, "That's where I'm going myself."

I was watching the boy so closely while I thought over this new situation that our eyes met; he gave me a quick smile. I was arguing: It is safer in here. If we could have planned it in this casual safe way, we should have done it like this. *It's quite private and quite safe in here. Talk to him!*

Things would have happened very differently if I had obeyed the impulse and asked him there and then, "Can I get a ticket here for Roea?" But I recalled that our people had elaborate plans for watching over the meeting at the station. Also, there was the part Ingrid Quist had to play. So I held my peace, and after an interval paid my bill and left the café.

I left Frobisher at his table. The waitress had come over to talk, and the last I saw of him he was glancing at his watch. I was much lighter in mind. I was convinced this was going to be all right, and as I crossed Stortingsgaten

toward the station I was telling myself, "You have a pleasant little surprise in store for the good-looking English boy
from the RAF when he finds he has been sitting next to his
contact in a café!"

I had four minutes to go when I entered the station.
There were groups of Germans about and two of them gave
me a close look as I turned down the stairs, but—to say the
least of that look—it was not hostile. The telephone booth
I had earlier decided on as the best for keeping an eye on
the ticket windows—the end one of three—was, of course,
occupied. A country woman and her parcels filled it to
bursting. But the next booth was empty, and it would do.
I entered and closed the door behind me, taking up a position with the receiver in my hand so that I could see the
ticket windows out of the corner of my eye while at the
same time presenting only the back of my shoulders to the
public milling about the place.

I looked at my wrist watch. Almost time.

The instrument was making an insistent buzzing sound
in my ear, and my heart was beating so heavily I seemed
to hear that, too. All sorts of people seemed to come and
go in an endless stream and the fantastic idea came to me:
What would happen if suddenly all the people in a crowded
city like Oslo forgot where they were going?—where they
lived? It would take a thousand years to put the muddle
right and get each one in his own bed in his own bedroom,
in his own house, in his own street. When the mind is
keyed up it will think of the most extraordinary things
just to give itself something to do to fill in the intolerable
gap while nothing is happening.

Then I saw Frobisher. He came through the swinging

doors and crossed the hall quickly to the ticket office. He looked casually around as if he were waiting for a girl; equally casually he separated his rackets and began to spin one in his right hand. . . .

This was it, but I still had to wait. I had taken up this position in the booth for a special reason—a normal safety check in Resistance work, but one that seemed very cunning to me. I—the real contact who would have information of value to extract under torture—was to wait until someone had gone in first to test the water.

This innocent person—the "duck" as he was called—would genuinely have no idea what it was all about, and—if there was a trap—this fact would soon be apparent to the Germans, who had the art of questioning down to brutal perfection. It took courage to be the duck, but generally the worst that could happen would be a beating-up.

Nils's duck was Ingrid Quist, but she did not know it. I was watching out for the glamorous blond, and sure enough she came along, on time.

From my booth I saw her eyes go at once to the racket. She walked up to Frobisher, groping very realistically in her handbag for change to use at the ticket window for her supposed ticket to Roea. In front of Frobisher she pulled up short. . . .

This was where I stepped into the picture. My job was to make contact with the English boy and get rid of Ingrid Quist as soon as possible by giving her an appointment to call at a nonexistent house the next morning. Frobisher and I were then to have our talk together.

I was out of the telephone booth and passing the swinging doors on my way to join Frobisher and the girl when a clumsy man in a raincoat almost knocked me off my feet. He seemed in a great hurry, and before I recovered my balance entirely he had gone on. But he left a delayed impression on my mind suddenly which flashed over me. The arm that jostled me had been jerked out of the raincoat pocket, and *it was carrying an automatic pistol.*

My eyes shot to Frobisher and Ingrid Quist. The girl was already surrounded. The place seemed full of these men, who had come from nowhere. I could see her startled face, open-mouthed, as they pushed through the crowd taking her away. Frobisher, his tennis rackets under one arm, was talking to a German in uniform while they both watched the girl being taken. I must have hung there for some time, gaping idiotically, incapable of thought, when suddenly I remembered what Nils had impressed on me—to move fast in the first few seconds.

My stumble had brought me to the swinging doors. One side was slightly open under the pressure of my outflung arm. At that moment I heard the officer Frobisher was speaking to yell an order in German, and I fell through and raced up the stairs. As I left, a soldier appeared on the other side of the swinging doors, closing the exit against the people trapped there below. With German thoroughness they were going to see if any other Resistance people had been on hand at the rendezvous.

I climbed the rest of the stairs more slowly. It seemed to me strange that everything in the street above should be going on much as usual. I turned right, crossed Stortingsgaten, and took the streetcar as directed to the place where I was to meet Nils. I felt perfectly normal—in fact, very brave and keyed up for anything—until I got about halfway to Skippergaten on the streetcar. Then I had a struggle to prevent myself from being sick.

I was thinking: That nice-looking boy . . . and I thought he was English. If it hadn't been for the careful way Nils and the others planned, you would be the one on the way to Victoria Terrasse now. . . .

The office in Skippergaten was above a shop. It had a small door and from the street level you went up a flight of stairs. Nils was waiting on these stairs for me—and when I told him what had happened we went no farther. Nils' face lost color. It was the only time I saw him like that. He took me straight out of the building again, to a car that was parked around the corner. The car ran on gasoline, not on a bag of coal gas attached to the roof or with a trailer that produced gas out of wood, so I expect it was a vehicle the Germans had not yet missed and thus was not exactly a safe conveyance to use at that time.

24

OUT

"WHERE ARE we going?"

"We're going out of this place—as fast as we can make it," Nils told me. "We can't afford to take any chances. But it's all been taken care of. You don't have to worry about a thing."

"What's been taken care of?" The little car was bouncing and lurching over the cobbled surface of the street so that I had to hold on to prevent myself being thrown about. Between two persons who know each other well there can be something in the atmosphere which conveys itself in a way no words can. I knew instinctively that Nils was nervous, and I knew before he said it what he was going to tell me.

"You will be taken over the border."

"Leave . . . my home?"

In a stupid way I could only think of the clothes I had left carelessly in the bedroom, of Kirsti's thermos bottle I should have scalded out that morning but had forgotten. "I would never be able to get ready in time."

217

Nils turned the car into the main road and tooted loudly at a van in his way. It was full of Germans, and the driver leaned out to snarl at us. When that little interlude was over, he said, "You're on your way now."

"You mean—we're not going back to my apartment?"

"It is the one place in Oslo—in all Norway—to keep away from."

"But I've got to get my things! I can't simply leave like this! It's impossible!"

"The impossible is easy when you try," Nils said. "Just sit tight and if no one tries to stop us we'll be out of this town in no time at all. You're lucky to have Hjoerdis and the others to look after your place for you. They'll see to everything until you get back."

"Kirsti!" I said. "How are you going to get her?"

"Same way as I'm getting you. Don't worry so about things. It's routine, now. If anything goes wrong we let certain people know and they take on whoever it is has to disappear for a while. They'll see you and Kirsti safely into Sweden. They have guides."

A traffic policeman stopped us at a crossroad. As we drew up he turned and appeared to give me a close scrutiny. I felt sure he was going to poke his head inside and ask me where I was going and what I was doing. The Quisling police were as bad as the Germans—at times more dangerous, because where you could fool a German, especially in regard to local knowledge, you could not always convince a Quisling policeman. As soon as he began to move aside, waving us on, Nils let in the clutch and contemptuously crowded him out of our way, narrowly missing his foot. The man shouted something in Norwegian; Nils swore back at him. All this began to have an effect on my nerves. It seemed stupid to act so conspicuously and foolhardily. It was clearly inviting trouble.

"Why not get Kirsti now?" I asked.

"I'm not going to let you go back anywhere near the apartment, in the first place. In the second place, I am not going to waste any time in getting you out of reach. And lastly, I'll get you safe first, then get Kirsti, instead of risking having you both caught in one swoop. Now relax. We have a long way to go."

Nils drove me out to a farm in Aurskog that night. Possibly it was because he drove at policemen, as if he were a German, and swore at troops, as if he were someone in authority; possibly, it was just luck, but we were only stopped once on the journey and that was at a bridge. A young Norwegian was on guard there against sabotage and he must have been a decent sort. He read Nils's pass for the Oslo district and waved us through, though we had no right to be there and no right to be using the car we were in. The Germans had a system whereby young men, civilians, were forced to patrol the railways, a group to each sector throughout the entire length of the line, and if the Resistance men blew up the line, the group in whose sector the damage occurred were shot. The Norwegians called this *borgevakt,* and it cost hundreds of fine young Norwegians their lives—shot up against a wall.

Nils evidently had been out to this farm in the hills before, for he knew his way about. The farmhouse lay back from a third-class country road which was more of a track than a highway, and as far as I knew there was no village or township closer than Soerumsand, itself no metropolis.

It was a horrible, desolate spot, at the back end of nowhere, with no lights showing. Only the fierce barking of the farm dogs indicated that human beings lived here. Nils left me in the car and knocked at a door in the pitch darkness. After a while someone asked him questions, and he answered, and then I heard the sound of a door being unbolted. He came back to the car and fetched me out to meet Fru Tollefsen, who had greeted him warmly.

A log fire was burning in the open grate in a long, low room. On the center table a supper of porridge was laid out —in the hills Norwegians live close to the survival line, for the living standard could hardly be lower. Tollefsen was sitting at the table in his suspenders, his heavy farm boots drying beside the hearth. He rose at once to greet Nils.

"Fru Tollefsen is the first link on the road out for a lot of us," Nils said to me, then turned to the farmer's wife. "Aren't you, Fru Tollefsen?"

"I do what I can," she said. "They come at all hours."

"And go!" Nils winked at me. He was trying hard to be cheerful. "You remember Herr Hirschfeldt and the lady and the little girl?"

"I remember them. We get important people through sometimes, and so cultured."

I thought: This category obviously does not include me. "Fru Hirschfeldt was my friend," I said. I suddenly felt ravenously hungry. Even the bread and the gruel on that table looked good to me.

"This lady has a little girl like Sara Hirschfeldt. I'm going to fetch her out here."

"Tonight?" the farmer asked.

"I'll be back with Kirsti before you know it." Nils blew

on his hands and rubbed them briskly together before taking up a glass of aquavit the farmer offered him. "Meanwhile, look after Fru Astrup and give her something to eat
and a warm bed, eh? Next thing she knows I'll be waking
her up to put the little girl in bed with her. Her troubles
are now all over. So—*adjoe!*"

I heard the door bolts being shot again and the sound of
the little car grinding off down the farm track, and there
was a lump in my throat that prevented me from speaking.
Nils was one of the kindest men at heart that I ever hope
to meet.

War is like a giant machine that comes to take away
such men, each time leaving the world coarser. I must tell
you now that, in the end, it took Nils. He was executed by
the Germans. I don't think he expected anything else.
Sooner or later. I was a thousand miles away at the time, and
of course did not know of it; but it is still my regret I could
not have been there to be of some comfort to him, to give
some small return for all the courage he gave to me.

Fru Tollefsen fussed over me like an old hen, and after
a wash and time to recover my composure I was sitting
down to *speke skinke* and greens with a will. Later I retired to the huge feather bed in the back room overlooking
the pines and the cowsheds, and it seemed that I had only
just closed my eyes when I felt someone pulling roughly at
my shoulder. It was Nils, in his arms a heavenly, drowsy,
sleepy-eyed bundle with two-colored hair spilling out all
over the warm blanket that wrapped her—*Kirsti!*

"Nils brought me," she said in Norwegian, and was fast
asleep again. I took her and held her close against my side

in that huge bed. My heart was overflowing, but when I tried to say something to Nils I found he was gone.

That was the last I ever saw of Nils Berg.

I slept late the next morning; Kirsti was up long before me. She dressed without disturbing me and lost no time in making herself at home with the farmer, so that when I eventually awoke to find the sun high and the valley sparkling Kirsti was able to give me all sorts of information about the place, including thumbnail biographies of the cows. Later, she managed to get herself shut in the primitive "three-seater" at the back and was there for half an hour unperturbed—something was always happening with Kirsti!

I tried to give Fru Tollefsen a hand during the morning while we awaited "Olaf," for whom the farmer had sent to take charge of us. The weirdest-looking man ever arrived soon after we had eaten a midday meal that made even our supper of the night before look lavish. He sat with his hands between his knees in the kitchen and waited without a word, looking like something out of the Middle Ages —a dim-witted camp-follower of the time of King Alfred, for instance.

This was Olaf, who may or may not have been dim-witted, but who did a very useful job by taking parties over the hills some thirty miles nearer to the frontier. These were difficult miles unless you knew where the Germans were. They controlled most of the normal routes, but if you knew how to avoid these—and this was not easy in mountain country—the risks were slight. Olaf had a peculiar haircut, straight across his forehead. His hair was straw-colored and grew in lank tufts behind the fringe, which only served to strengthen in him the suggestion of a troll. He had ears that stuck out—indeed, came actually just a little bit forward—which he could move like a horse while twitching his other face muscles. The mournful eyes were like those of a St. Bernard dog, only of the palest gray. His cheeks were blue-black with stubble, and over-all he must have been about six feet six in height, with legs almost the same shape all the way down to a pair of enormous feet.

Olaf fascinated Kirsti. She could scarcely take her eyes off him as we followed the track over the pastures at the back of the farm. I made a grateful farewell to Fru Tollefsen, but there was little I could offer except words. The pair of them took this business as a matter of course, and they did it simply because they loved their country and hated the Germans. There were many in Norway like the Tollefsens. If a country has a backbone of that quality you can never break it.

We started in a short belt of pine trees, but soon came out into the close-cropped, rolling pasture of the hills. The larks were singing in the afternoon sun, and the butterflies and the horseflies—which you get all over the countryside in Norway—darted about the carpet of flowers. Those small puff-like snowballs of cloud so characteristic of the country rode the sky against a deep-blue background. It was a lovely day, the sort that remains in your memory, and there was not a soul to be seen on the way. We had the whole hillside and the whole glorious day to ourselves. Oslo and the Germans seemed a thousand miles away.

Our guide and protector walked stolidly on ahead, one pace to two of mine and three of Kirsti's. He never looked back to see if we were still there and he never uttered a word. When after about two hours' march we came to a primitive log bridge over a gully, he stopped in the center and stood there, reaching out to hand us one by one safely across. Then he moved his legs like a crane again, got ahead in half a dozen strides, and strict protocol was thereafter observed—in silence, of course. We walked until about nine-thirty—it was still broad daylight—then Olaf took us up a sharp incline that led to a natural balconylike shelf in the mountainside. Here among the trees was a hut with bunks and a stove for cooking. I made cocoa and heated the food Olaf carried. We ate in silence, and afterward Kirsti and I wrapped ourselves in the blankets provided by the Resistance and slept like logs, with Olaf outside on the veranda in spite of the nip in the air.

We moved off early next day.

I knew we were due to reach the last lap in Westmarka and get within striking distance of the frontier and the road to Charlottenberg sometime that afternoon, and Olaf wasted no time. Perhaps he had another job to do. I do not know. Perhaps I know simply nothing about him, for he made no remark of any sort. He might have been dumb for all we knew.

We arrived at another farm shortly after midday. This lay at the end of a fertile valley and, like the last, was lost in the hills. I don't know how even the country folk who lived there could find it. It was near no village that I saw, and there was no road, apart from a track, for miles. Olaf walked in the gates quite openly, and we tramped across the yard and straight into a rough sort of barn that had been a cowshed. A woman was peeling potatoes into a bucket in the black shadows by the wide doors, and when she looked up sharply I got a shock. I could have asked her how her baby was—but I didn't. She was the woman at the sink who had said good-night to me when I was leaving Anders Evensen's house in a great hurry. She smiled at me now, and when I looked around for our medieval mute he was gone.

"Find a corner," the woman said. "There's lots of room and it's quite comfortable in the straw. No matches or lights, but otherwise do as you like."

"How long have you been here?" I asked her. Apparently she did not recognize me, although of course she might suddenly remember. I decided to rely on the Resistance principle and say nothing.

"A long time," the woman said. "It's not bad, and they say we're off soon."

I knew better than to ask any more questions.

Soon Kirsti and I were resting our aching limbs in a neat little nest we made in the straw. Kirsti went off to sleep almost at once. She had a marvelous constitution for a child. She had stood up to the long trek over the hills and along the valleys without a murmur. Even at that age she could eat almost as much as I.

After a while a woman I had never seen before asked if we would like some soup, so I woke Kirsti and we went out into the yard at the back of the barn. Here a primitive cookhouse was installed, with a wood fire and an oven made out of an old oil drum. I saw nine women, three babies, and a boy—the boy who was in the party that surprised us at the Evensens' house. I recognized three or four of the women, and I also recognized Irma Jensen, who seemed to be in charge.

Kirsti and I each held out a bowl to be filled from the

steaming pot. We were given huge chunks of bread, and we followed the rest in dipping the bread into our soup and chewing at the mashy result. It was delicious. We spent three days at the farm and all I can remember is the eating we did. Everyone ate all day long, one meal overlapping another. In gaps we filled up on soup and bread until a proper meal was ready. I got up in the middle of the night once because I thought I heard Germans creeping up on our little gypsylike settlement, only to find that several of our women were heating up a pot of stew and dispatching it. Apparently a five-hour break for sleep was too long to endure without eating. All of us, of course, had been half-starved for months, and Mother Nature was catching up.

But if anyone ate more than Kirsti I should be surprised. Irma Jensen said, on one occasion when she discovered Kirsti coming up for the third time in the line at the cooking pot, "She's already eaten twice her weight in food to-day. Why not three?"

On the fourth night the farmer and his brother came into the barn, and, after speaking with Irma Jensen, told us to be ready soon after dark. At this period it was not difficult, as it later became, to get over the frontier, provided you knew the ground. Then the Germans merely had machine-gun posts on certain routes along which people were known to escape, but by the end of the war they had a chain of such posts all along the frontier.

We were now only five and a half miles from the Swedish border, and any time we were liable to meet German troops who would shoot at once. Even women, the farmer told us. Irma Jensen spoke to me before we started that night. She knew me from my activities in distributing the newssheet, but she did not know anything else about me, although we were both workers in the movement. I knew she wouldn't ask me any questions. The fact that I was there was sufficient. I had to be got out.

"There are two parties here that should have gone over before now," Irma said. "You and Kirsti make a third. Some of these women are inclined to get panicky. Keep an eye on them. There are some that didn't like waiting about —poor dears! They've been through a lot."

I would have liked to ask what, but again I knew better. I promised to do anything I could to support morale, but I didn't see what could be expected of me. I was probably as frightened as any.

"We had an old man who died," Irma said.

I remembered the old man with the scarf in the hall at the Evensens'.

"He couldn't stand the journey and died in his sleep on the way. The poor chap was completely illiterate. He'd been a sailor during fifty-four years at sea, and he has to die at eighty-four in a mountain hut! The Germans sent to arrest him because he spat at a corporal in a streetcar, and then used a lot of indecent language—wasted it—on a Quisling policeman!"

I felt a great respect for the old sailor who had made his last voyage, and personally I think he finished in style. To spit at a German at eighty-four!

"I believe a guide was recently killed in the mountains by a patrol, and they don't like it. They've been waiting to see how the situation develops, and twice there have been false alarms about a start. Now we have all these women and we have to get the place clear. Another lot's coming up soon."

Women, babies, the boy, and Kirsti, we all set out, and for an hour we climbed out of the valley, with the farmer as our guide. There followed a long wait in the forest, as the dawn came closer with every passing minute. The woman with the two months' old baby began to weep; so Irma gave me the baby to hold while she told the mother she would soon be in Sweden, where there was plenty of milk. Nevertheless, morale began to drop, until two Norwegians arrived and went into conference with the farmer. Soon he left to return home, while the newcomers led on through the forest until we came to two huts. Here we passed the first night.

I shall never forget that week we spent almost within rifleshot of Sweden. Most of the women were factory workers who had refused to be deported to Germany and were about to be taken by force when the Resistance intervened. They were good sorts, but naturally not from the top level of intellect. Two were illiterate, and there was one young girl who I was surprised to hear had been employed at all. The Norwegians can produce great minds. They can also produce some of the dimmest. This girl Klara was from the latter group. At any moment, for no cause, she would start to howl like a wolf. This was sure to set someone else off, so Irma and I were busy.

On the fourth day the man who had been bringing us food and news came to say we had to go back to the farm. No one could be sent to show us the way out, and it was too dangerous for us to remain here, because the Germans had

been bringing troops into the area. The guides refused
to take any more across.

Irma called me in to share the news, but she did not pass
it on to the rest. It appeared that we were on our own without the prospect of any more supplies arriving. It looked as
if we had to return. But I was determined that, having
come so far, I personally was not going back. Kirsti and I
would try it ourselves—but we had all these women on our
hands, to say nothing of the babies and the boy, who seemed
to lack all spirit.

"We'll have to tell them in the morning—and set out
on our way back," Irma decided. She looked at me. "You
won't let me down?"

"I'll come back as far as the farm," I promised. There
was little else I could do. "But as soon as we get in sight of
the place I'm finding my way out myself."

"You couldn't do it by yourself."

"I'm not going back. I can't go back."

"They'll take care of us all," Irma said. "They never let
anyone down. You should know that."

I wondered how much she knew about me. Anyway, I
kept urging her, "Why don't you come along with us? It's
only the other side there." We could see some distant huts
among the pines that we knew were in Sweden, and there
seemed to be no roads, no houses, frontier post or any signs
of activity whatsoever. In between lay a gently falling slope
of pasture and a belt of forest pine, rough desolate country
not likely to be patrolled. "Two would be safer than one."

"If it's so easy there would be no reason for guides."

"You can't tell till you try. A woman can hide in the

forest as easily as a man. The Germans can't patrol every yard."

"I'm going to wait. They know best."

I decided to take a chance with this girl, for I was now convinced that we could get out together. "You brought some of these people out through Anders Evensen at Vettakollen, didn't you?" I asked. "The old man was with you then. He had a scarf around his head."

Irma stopped lacing her boot and looked at me uncertainly. "Yes, that is so," she said. "How did you know? About the scarf, I mean?"

I wanted her to have confidence in me, so I merely said, "I knew all about it. I was watching it. I was in the house when you came in that night. I saw you go upstairs to Anders."

"Well . . ." she said. "I only remembered you from delivering the newssheet. What was all this about?"

"That would be a long story," I answered. "Let's get back to our problems. I don't think you should turn back now. More people are coming up. We ought at least to make a try to get over. Why not give it a spin?"

"I might. Let me think of it a bit."

As it happened, Irma had already been turning over in her mind the idea of making a break. Too much trouble lay the other way. She had been picked up in Oslo by the Norwegian police, carrying a stack of Resistance newssheets in the saddlebag of her bicycle. How our people got her out of the hands of the Quislings and out of Oslo I never found out, but she was on her way toward the frontier within twenty-four hours of being arrested.

Irma and I told the women we were leaving next morn-

ing to return to the farm. I realize now that it was dangerous at that place with so many of us collected together for
no apparent reason. We left the forest very early, and as it
happened we had not gone far when we met the farmer
coming up to fetch us. He was in a very bad temper—poor
man! By now Irma had made up her mind to join me, and
we were glad to be relieved of our charges. As it happened
the whole lot was rounded up by a German corporal on a
motorcycle and shepherded into a police station the following afternoon. The guide they had with them escaped a
burst of fire the corporal sent to greet the party, and, with
the boy, got clean away. The women probably got sent to
Germany after all—at least I wished the Nazis joy of Klara.

Irma and I returned to the woods to collect our packs,
and then set out in the direction of the huts without delay.
My rucksack contained wool socks and clothing, Norwegian
money, some chocolate Jan had given me, a blanket and
some canned meat. Kirsti's contained only clothing.

As we came out of the forest onto the slope I suddenly
saw Irma in a detached sort of way—as a stranger would
see her—and I decided then that we would have to leave
the packs behind. They marked us as people who were
traveling, whereas, if stopped, our only hope would be to
pass ourselves off as local women going about our normal
business. Here Kirsti would help, because no one would
expect a little girl to be on the run from the security police.

I managed to convince Irma, and we abandoned our
gear with regret. I thought then how right Nils had been
when he advised against my carrying my hoard of gold with
me when I took to flight. He said it was safer hidden away
in my bathroom. Hjoerdis would look after it.

So we set out on the last lap with nothing at all except the clothes we were wearing. With Kirsti, we made an innocent trio. Irma certainly looked like a healthy, robust country girl, and that I myself looked far from elegant had been made clear enough by Fru Tollefsen.

We walked straight across the pasture until we came to a stone wall, on the other side of which was a farm track. Up and down the valley there still was nothing in sight, but marks of heavy motor tires showed in the turf of the track. We followed these tread marks for a while, since they led us in the general direction of the huts, and so reached a spot from which we could see German soldiers erecting a hut in a bend made by a stream. We struck off at right angles, to the north away from the Germans, following the bank of the stream. We had an idea that it might be Sweden on the far side, but we did not want to risk being seen by the troops. We walked on.

Eventually we came to a bridge where a smaller stream joined the larger. This was cultivated land, and it was likely that there would be buildings somewhere near. We crossed the bridge, as it happened arguing together about the food parcels the Swedes sent out for Norwegian children, when I suddenly noticed a look of horror on Irma's face. Then I myself saw that a German sergeant was standing at my elbow. Some half a dozen German soldiers were sitting on a wall in the sun, smoking and taking it easy. It was a lesson —especially to women—not to talk, but I was not occupied with lessons then. I was trying to think what came next.

We had no papers. We were close to the frontier. We had no right to be there, and possibly less local knowledge than these German youths. Luckily, the sergeant with his very first word gave us a loophole. He said, *"Allo!* And where are *you* going?"

The *allo* put us on the level of local girls, with whom these youths were evidently in the habit of trying out their Norwegian, so I said, "Wouldn't you like to know!"

Irma told me afterward she was so frightened by the sight of all these Germans rising and coming in around us that she could not do a thing, not even stop walking. And this was lucky again, for I kept on walking, too, and so did Kirsti.

"Hey!" the sergeant yelled. "Aren't you going to stop and talk?"

"Not likely!" I called back. I think that a sudden bang would have started us off on a dead run, but nothing happened except that one of the boys said something in German I could not catch, which set them all laughing.

Around the bend was a farm building, but luckily no one was in sight and we made our way safely into a wood. . . .

This was the only danger we met, as it happened, among the much-vaunted perils of this journey, for shortly afterward we saw an old man eating his lunch in a corner of a field. He was obviously a farm worker—probably, in these parts, the small farmer himself—and he had obviously just finished his morning's work. In addition, there was something reassuring in the steady, vacant-eyed way he ate his bread. I left the others in concealment and went over to talk to him. He showed no surprise when I told him I was trying to get into Sweden. I expect he was used to the situation, for he told me his farm was on the border and that I only had to walk through the trees at the bottom and I would be in Sweden.

"You'll see a church on the hill in the far distance when you come out of the pines," he said. "Walk straight toward it along the stream and you'll come to a village, and if you go carefully until you get to the village you'll be all right. The Swedish guard here is an old chap with a temper and he likes to stick to formalities, but in the village you'll be all right."

I thanked him and went back to tell Irma.

We did as he said, and we saw the church, and we made the village, and there my story must end.

AFTERWORD

AFTER HER ESCAPE via Sweden, Helen Astrup stayed with relatives in London for a while, working for the Norwegian government which was then established there. Her health broke down and she retired to Bath to convalesce. From this time she had nothing more to do with work for the Norwegians. Kirsti was sent to school in Bath and soon it was impossible to tell her from a dozen other little girls fluttering about Lansdown Crescent. She and her mother saw the war out in the West Country, then came to live in Sloane Street in London.

After the war Hjoerdis visited England and stayed in Bath with Helen. She returned to marry a Norwegian to whom she had once been engaged. At that time, she changed her mind; but later this fighter pilot escaped from a POW camp and Hjoerdis changed her mind again when she met him in London. She now has two babies and lives in Oslo. Her husband has a job with the shipping line owned by Carsten Astrup's relatives. Kirsti has spent several holidays with Hjoerdis and her growing family, one of the attractions being that she rates a free passage at any time from Bristol to Oslo in the company's ships.

The Norwegian patriot Helen calls Nils was shot by the Germans when they turned up his real identity. A man might escape the first time. He might get away half a dozen times. But anyone who kept on was bound to be caught in the end. Most of those Norwegian underground workers knew this. Nils was a good man and a very likeable chap.

The girl Irma, with whom Helen escaped from Norway, is at this time working in Washington as a translator. For a while she had a similar job with the United Nations.

Several attempts have been made to find the *Leonora.* At one period Mrs. Astrup was pestered with letters from people who wished to finance her and share the spoils. In this narrative the place-names around Larkollen (which you can locate on the maps of Norway) have been made confusing on purpose, to discourage treasure hunters. If the Norwegian Navy cannot find the wreck it is not likely that an amateur will be able to chance on the spot. What brought on the spate of inquiries was the unearthing of a large part of the rest of the stolen bullion in Oslo itself shortly after the end of the war in Europe. People are still looking for the *Leonora,* however. If she is ever found the fate of Jan may be decided. I have heard now a good deal more of the story than appears in print in this book. I have listened to several sides of the affair as distinct from Helen's. I believe Jan was too badly hurt to have survived for long. I have walked along that jetty and it is obvious that anyone in the barn would have the fighting edge over an opponent in the open. In the clear light of early morning, silhouetted against the water of the fjord, Jan must have been a sitting duck for the men in the barn. There is no doubt that when he eventually got back to the *Leonora* he was done for. If a craft has been crashed into jetties and torn out again, and in addition splintered by direct rifle fire, it is not likely to be—to say the least of it—a seaworthy boat. My guess is that the *Leonora* plugged on, sinking lower and lower in the water, with two dead men aboard. Then she sank and took the gold with her to the bottom of the sea.

— B.L.J.

About the Authors

HELEN ASTRUP's biography has been substantially given in the preceding pages, particularly in the first and sixth chapters and in the Foreword.

BERNARD LOUIS JACOT DE BOINOD (B. L. Jacot) is British but has strong ties of blood across the Channel—a French father, and a great-great-grandfather who was one of Napoleon's generals (the rue de Boinod in Paris honors his name). Mr. Jacot, born in England on February 25, 1899, was educated at King Edward's School, Birmingham, and King's College, Oxford. He played football for England while at Oxford, and also swam in the 100 meters at the Olympic Games. A varied career followed, including a period as barrister-at-law of the Inner Temple, a stint on *The Times* of London, and assignments as European correspondent for the New York *Herald Tribune* and deputy editor of the London *News-Chronicle*. He also put in some time as a Hollywood script writer for Metro-Goldwyn-Mayer. Mr. Jacot has written a great deal professionally, specializing in the short story; examples of his work have appeared in *Punch, The New Yorker, Collier's, The Atlantic Monthly,* and *The Saturday Evening Post,* and have been collected into several books. During the war Mr. Jacot was both a pilot in the RAF and a full colonel in the United States Army Air Force; some mention of his career is made in his own Foreword, and it may also be added that he was wounded in the evacuation of Dunkirk. He lives at the present time at Radstock in Somerset, where two particular hobbies are playing Chopin and breeding dachshunds (he owns the current English Champion of Champions, "Edith").